The INDOOR Electric GRILL COOKBOOK

101 Delicious Recipes Plus Pro Tips
& Illustrated Instructions!

By
Matt Jason

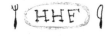

HHF Press
San Francisco

Editor: HHF Press

Art Direction: HHF Press

Illustrations: HHF Press

All photographs in this book © HHF Press or © Depositphotos.com

Published in the United States of America by HHF Press

268 Bush St, #3042

San Francisco, CA 94104 USA

www.HHFPress.com

Contents

Seafood 94

Breads and Sandwiches.............. 128

About

Indoor Grills

What Does an Indoor Grill Do?

The indoor grill is a revolutionary device because it allows you the freedom to grill all of your favorite foods any time of year. No matter the weather outside, you can prepare delicious grilled food whenever you want.

Indoor grills give you maximum flexibility because they allow you to grill indoors without excessive smoke. That's right, indoor grills actually draw smoke in, allowing you to safely cook indoors all year.

Regardless of what you want to cook, you can be sure that your fast-heating indoor grill will give you the perfectly grilled results you expect with the convenience of cooking on the stove. Because of the way indoor grills are designed, you will also see some impressive health benefits when using an indoor grill.

Since indoor grills work using electricity rather than gas or charcoal, this means faster, cleaner cooking no matter what you choose to grill. Non-stick grilling surfaces mean you don't have to worry about food sticking to the grill, and precise temperature controls mean you don't have to worry about the grill being too hot or too cold.

Best of all, avoiding charcoal means your food will be healthier, safer, and easier to cook than ever. Cleanup is quick and easier thanks to the non-stick, removable cooking surface, and storage takes only a fraction of the space of a normal outdoor grill.

Who is an Indoor Grill Good For?

Because indoor grills are so compact and so easy to use, it's good for anyone who wants the flavor of authentic grilled food without having to cook outside with charcoal or gas. Just like with regular grills, you will have the flexibility to cook different foods at the same time, and you will still get that unmistakable grilled flavor with everything you cook.

These grills are also especially helpful for grilling enthusiasts who find themselves living in apartments where space for an outdoor grill just isn't an option.

But indoor grills are also great as an addition to your traditional grill. If there are times when you want to be able to grill food quickly and easily without the hassle of warming up the grill and scrubbing afterwards, an indoor grill is perfect for you.

Who is it Not Good For?

While an indoor grill may be perfect for some, you will still need adequate ventilation in order for the grill to work properly. If your cooking space doesn't offer any sort of ventilation at all, an indoor grill may not work for you.

A Few Cautions

All grills share one thing in common: They get hot. When using your indoor grill, you always want to make sure that you are aware of whether your grill is turned on. While indoor grills to take a few minutes to heat up, you should always assume that the grill is hot anytime it is turned on.

Always make sure that children are well supervised around your indoor grill, and make sure to turn off your grill as soon as you are finished using it.

Did You Know...?

You may not be surprised to hear that grilling food is a pretty old technique. In fact, it goes back over a half a million years. Early humans found that meat cooked over fire was actually more nutritious than raw meat. The reason? Bioavailability. In short, cooking meat changes the structure of proteins and fats allowing them to be more efficiently digested and absorbed by the body. Until the 1940s grilling was mostly something that people did around campfires, but after World War II and the expansion of suburbs, the popularity of backyard grilling skyrocketed. By the 1950s the backyard BBQ was a staple of family entertaining, and it remains this way today.

Matt Jason

2

How to Use
Your Indoor Grill

Setting Up the Grill

When you remove the grill from its packaging, you will notice that all of the parts are marked as either "dishwasher safe" or "not dishwasher safe." In order to make sure all of the grill components continue to work properly you must make sure that only "dishwasher safe" parts are washed in the dishwasher.

Install the drip pan into the base of the grill before installing the grilling surface. Place the base of the grill on a flat surface and place the cooking surface on the base. Attach the power cable to the grill and plug the cord into a grounded outlet (three prong). Your grill is now ready for use.

Learning the Controls

Most indoor grills only feature one simple temperature control, and this is really all you need in order grill anything. Typically, indoor grills have a temperature range of 200 F to 450 F and this should be sufficient for cooking nearly anything.

The simplicity of the controls on an indoor grill means you can be ready to cook in minutes.

The Grilling Process

Once you have turned on your indoor grill, you need to wait for a few minutes for the grill to come to the desired temperature. Most grills will be fully heated after about five minutes.

Because your indoor grill's cooking surface is coated in a non-stick material, there is no need to use cooking spray or any other type of cooking fat. In fact, most grills should not be used with any kind of oil because this can cause unwanted buildup over time that will hurt the non-stick surface.

Once your grill is hot enough for cooking, you can add food to it. Because the grill is single sided, you will still need to flip your food as it cooks. The excess fat from cooking will drip down to the drip pan located under the cooking surface. It is important to empty the drip pan after each use.

When you have finished cooking and food has been removed from the grill, turn the grill off immediately. Before disassembling the grill, make sure it is unplugged and completely cool. Use a wet cloth or sponge to clean the cooking surface, and make sure the drip pan is empty before storing the grill.

Health Benefits of Indoor Grilling

Foods (Meat and Vegetables) Retain More Nutrients

Unlike other forms of cooking like frying or boiling which pull nutrients out of the food, grilling seals more nutrients into the food. That means that your vegetables retain more of their vitamins and meats keep more nutrients like riboflavin and thiamine, all of which are important for a healthy diet.

No Cancer Causing Chemicals

First, the fact that you don't need to add any kind of lubricant to an indoor grill means that you will never have to worry about what may be in your cooking spray. Some studies have suggested that the blackened, burned parts of grilled foods may change the structure of the meat and release cancer-causing free radicals. By gently grilling foods on your indoor grill, you don't need to worry about this potential hazard.

No Smoke or Carbon Monoxide

Unlike traditional grilling or even pan cooking on a stove top, this method of cooking does not release a lot of smoke or harmful carbon monoxide. Only a small amount of steam will escape the food as it cooks. This form of cooking is incredibly safe and will not bother people with upper respiratory issues.

No Charcoal

Charcoal grilling has been the standard for many years, but it carries a whole host of risks. Did you know that cooking with charcoal also increases your risk of cancer? The combination of charcoal, lighter fluid, and dripping fats causes a variety of compounds that are considered carcinogenic. And you're not just breathing these chemicals when you cook. They're actually coating your food! Charcoal grills also contribute to air pollution by releasing large amounts of carbon monoxide and carbon dioxide into the atmosphere. An indoor grill does not carry any of these risks.

CHAPTER

3

Pro Tips

Avoid Abrasive Materials on Your Grill

The last thing that you want to do is destroy your brand-new grill so it is important to know what common household items could do just that. Start by avoiding butter or oil sprays on the non-stick surface. Not only can these additives add calories to your meal, but they can destroy your non-stick surface—the grill instructions specifically say to avoid using cooking sprays. It is wise to avoid the use of abrasive cleaning materials which can also strip the non-stick surface.

Be Prepared with All the Essential Grilling Equipment

Don't be fooled into thinking that just because it sits on your countertop that this isn't a legitimate grill. This is a real grill that lets you grill almost anything you would grill on a traditional flame grill so you will need the same tools that you use on a traditional grill. However—never use metal utensils on the grill, as this is a surefire way to destroy the grill plates, and in turn, your grill. Make sure that you are prepared with all the essentials, and be sure that they are wooden, silicone, or plastic to avoid damaging the grill.

Recreate the Taste of Traditional Grilling By Using Marinades

If anyone were to have a legitimate complaint about indoor grilling it would have to be that it just doesn't have the same taste as grilling over charcoal or smoking over wood chips. Luckily, there are a handful of companies out there that sell pre-made marinades that give your proteins that smoky flavor that you are missing out on. If you don't want to spend the money on a pre-made marinade, there are plenty of recipes out there to make your own smoky marinade to get all the health benefits of using your indoor grill without missing out on the outdoor grilling flavor.

Use Parchment Paper and Foil to Avoid Having to Clean Every Time

Let's face it, if you are using your grill every day (sometimes more than once) it will become tedious and make you not want to continue using the grill. A few standard kitchen materials are all it takes to get around having to clean every single time. First, wrap a piece of foil around the drip tin, when you are done you can simply roll the foil up and around the mess, then toss it. Secondly, grab a piece of parchment paper and lay it on the grill with the tear sides facing you. Slip your food in between the sheets and cook. Since it is parchment paper you don't need to worry about a fire hazard and the heat transfers nicely to cook the food in the same amount of time. When you are done you can just throw away the paper and your grill will look like it has never been used. Warning: Just make sure not to use parchment paper if grilling over 450 degrees or the paper may burn.

Avoid Creating Smoke by Prepping Your Meat Correctly

While cooking on an indoor grill does not inherently create smoke like grilling with fire does, there are a few ways that smoke can be created by grilling. First, cut off any excess fat.

Not only will this prevent the fat from smoking while cooking, but it will also make your meal healthier. You are also going to want to dry off any excess marinade and make sure that there is no seasoning left on the protein before you grill it. Herbs and spices like thyme, oregano, mustard seed, can cause a lot of smoke if heat is applied to them directly.

Keep a Spray Bottle of Apple Juice Handy

This may seem like a weird one, but believe me, you will love the results. Spraying your beef with a little apple juice before and during cooking helps it to keep its color and flavor. This works on any kind of beef from burgers to ribs and will add an extra flair to your next meal.

Matt Jason

Want a Personal 24/7 Cooking Coach?

Learn New Recipes & Techniques for FREE!

CHAPTER

4

Grilled
Fruits/Vegetables

Cinnamon Grilled Pineapple

Servings: 6 | Prep Time: 10 Minutes | Cook Time: 20 Minutes

This makes a delicious healthy dessert. The sweetness of the pineapple is paired with the warm flavor of the cinnamon.

Ingredients:

1 pineapple

2 teaspoons cinnamon

Directions:

1. Cut up the pineapple lengthwise into 2-inch-thick strips. Preheat the grill to medium-low heat.

2. Place the pieces onto skewers.

3. Season the pineapple with the cinnamon.

4. Grill the pineapple for 15 to 20 minutes, flipping once halfway through.

5. Serve immediately.

Nutritional Info: Calories: 190 | Sodium: 5 mg | Dietary Fiber: 5.7 g | Total Fat: 0.5 g | Total Carbs: 50.2 g | Protein: 2.1 g.

Balsamic Grilled Vegetable

This is an incredibly simply, and fast side dish. The balsamic and herbs give this dish a wonderful Italian flavor. You can use whatever vegetables you have on hand.

Ingredients:

1 pound zucchini

1 pound bell peppers

1 large red or white onion

1/3 cup Italian parsley or basil

Cooking spray

Balsamic Dressing:

2 tablespoons extra-virgin olive oil

2 tablespoons balsamic vinegar

2 garlic cloves

1 teaspoon salt

1/2 teaspoon ground black pepper

Directions:

1. Cut the zucchini in half lengthwise and then into 1/2-inch-thick pieces. Cut the bell pepper into strips. Cut the onion into 1/2-inch-thick rounds. Crush the garlic cloves. Spray the grill with cooking spray and preheat it on low heat.

2. Use a whisk to combine the balsamic dressing ingredients in a bowl.

3. Grill the vegetables for 6 minutes. Flip them over and grill for another 6 minutes. The vegetables should be tender when ready.

4. Once done, place the vegetable in a big bowl and cover with the balsamic dressing. Toss until well coated.

5. The vegetables can be served hot or cold. The vegetables can be stored in the refrigerator, in an airtight container for 3 to 4 days.

Nutritional Info: Calories: 90 | Sodium: 402 mg | Dietary Fiber: 3.1 g | Total Fat: 5.1 g | Total Carbs: 10.1 g | Protein: 2.1 g.

Ginger Sesame Grilled Tofu Steaks

Servings: 4 | Prep Time: 60 Minutes | Cook Time: 4 Minutes

The ginger sesame vinaigrette gives the tofu a spicy and nutty taste. Allowing the tofu to drain before marinating allows it to absorb more marinade.

Ingredients:

1 pound reduced-fat extra firm water-packed tofu, drained and cut crosswise into 8 slices

2/3 cups ginger-sesame vinaigrette (store bought or homemade)

1 tablespoon finely chopped fresh cilantro

1 tablespoon low-sodium soy sauce

8 lime slices

Cooking spray

2 cups hot cooked short-grain white rice

Directions:

1. Slice the tofu into 8 pieces crosswise. Put a few paper towels under the tofu and a few on top. Let the tofu rest for 20 minutes, pushing down on it from time to time. Chop the cilantro.

2. Mix the ginger sesame vinaigrette, soy sauce, and cilantro in a baking dish. Reserve 1/4 cup of it for later. Add in the tofu to the baking dish making sure they're in a single layer. Coat the tofu with the marinade. Flip them a few times to make sure they're well coated. Refrigerate the dish, covered, for 30 minutes. Flip the tofu from time to time.

3. While the tofu is marinating, preheat your grill to medium-high heat. Lightly grease the grill.

4. Coat the limes with the marinade. Place both the tofu and lime on the grill, keep the marinade. Grill both for 4 minutes, flipping halfway through. Coat both with the reserved marinade throughout. The tofu will brown when it's ready.

5. Divide the rice among 4 plates. Then top that with the tofu, and lime. Sprinkle some of the reserved marinade on top of the plates, and serve.

Nutritional Info: Calories: 439 | Sodium: 232 mg | Dietary Fiber: 2.3 g | Total Fat: 23.9 g | Total Carbs: 45.3 g | Protein: 13.3 g.

Grilled Apricots with Brie Prosciutto and Honey

Servings: 10 | Prep Time: 10 Minutes | Cook Time: 3 Minutes

You may not think about grilling apricots, but the turn out delicious. The brie, prosciutto, and honey make these apricots both salty, and sweet.

Ingredients:

> 5 apricots
> 4 slices of prosciutto
> 10 small wedges of brie cheese (approximately 2 ounces)
> Honey for drizzling on top

Directions:

1. Cut the apricots in half. Cut the prosciutto into 3 equal pieces, and then roll them into cylinders. Make sure the brie is room temperature. Preheat the grill to medium-high heat.

2. Use a brush to lightly coat the cut side of the apricots with oil.

3. Grill the apricots with the cut side down for about 3 minutes. The apricots should be a little soft. Put the apricots on a plate

4. Top the apricots with a piece of brie first, and then a piece of prosciutto. Drizzle desired amount of honey on the apricots. Drizzle more honey if you want the apricots to be on the sweeter side.

5. Serve immediately.

Nutritional Info: Calories: 77 | Sodium: 208 mg | Dietary Fiber: 0.0 g | Total Fat: 5.3 g | Total Carbs: 2.1 g | Protein: 5.5 g.

Grilled Artichoke

Servings: 4 | Prep Time: 15 Minutes | Cook Time: 45 Minutes

Grilling the artichoke gives it a little smokiness. The lemon juice compliments the flavor of the artichoke well.

Ingredients:

1 tablespoon fresh herbs such as rosemary, oregano, thyme	1 bay leaf
1/3 cup olive oil	1 lemon
2 cloves garlic	2 to 4 large globe artichokes
	Salt

Directions:

1. Chop the fresh herbs. Cut the garlic cloves in half. Cut the lemon into wedges.

2. Put the herbs in a microwave safe bowl, and add enough olive oil to cover the herbs. Place the bowl in the microwave and cook for 30 seconds on high. Set aside.

3. Fill a big pot with an inch of water. Put in the bay leaf, garlic cloves, and a steaming rack.

4. Use scissors to trim the pointy ends of the artichoke leaves. Rub the cut ends with the lemon wedges. Cut away the outer layer of the artichoke stem with a vegetable peeler. Cut the stem down so that it's 2 inches long.

5. Slice off and throw out the top 1/2-inch of the artichokes. Then slice the artichokes in half. Scoop out the small inside leaves, and the fuzzy parts using a metal spoon. Cover the insides with lemon juice.

6. Bring the water in the pot to a boil, and then reduce to medium-high heat. Put the artichokes with the cut side down in the steam rack.

7. Cover the pot, and steam the artichoke for about 20 minutes. The outer leaves should pull off easily when the artichoke is ready. Towards the end of the steaming process preheat your grill to high.

8. Brush the entire artichoke with herb oil and salt to taste. Put cut side of the artichoke on the grill, and grill for 5 to 10 minutes.

9. Serve with another sprinkling of lemon juice.

Nutritional Info: Calories: 231 | Sodium: 192 mg | Dietary Fiber: 9.6 g | Total Fat: 17.2 g | Total Carbs: 20.0 g | Protein: 5.7 g.

Grilled Brussels Sprout Skewers

Servings: 4 | Prep Time: 20 Minutes | Cook Time: 14 Minutes

The grilling gives these Brussels sprouts a nice smoky flavor. The balsamic reduction balances out the strong flavor of the Brussels sprouts

Ingredients:

1-pound brussels sprouts

1 tablespoon olive oil

Salt & pepper to taste

1 batch balsamic reduction

Directions:

1. Boil a big pot of water. Place the brussels sprouts in the water for about 3 to 4 minutes. Then place them in a colander and run them under cold water.

2. Cut off any long stems, and discard any loose leaves. Pat the sprouts dry gently.

3. In a bowl, toss the brussels sprouts with salt, pepper, and olive oil.

4. Preheat the grill to medium heat. Put 3 to 4 brussels sprouts on a skewer, and repeat until all the sprouts are used.

5. Grill the brussels sprouts for 4 to 5 minutes per side. All sides should have a char.

6. Place the skewers on a serving platter, and sprinkle them with the balsamic reduction.

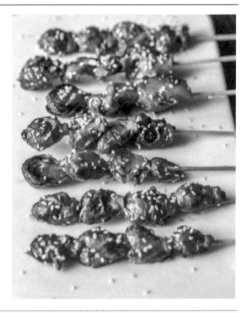

Nutritional Info: Calories: 80 | Sodium: 67 mg | Dietary Fiber: 4.3 g | Total Fat: 3.9 g | Total Carbs: 10.4 g | Protein: 3.9 g.

Grilled Cauliflower "Steaks"

Servings: 4 | Prep Time: 12 Minutes | Cook Time: 14 Minutes

This is an easy, fun side to serve at your next barbeque. The cauliflower grills up nicely, and gets a nice flavor from the seasoning.

Ingredients:

2 heads cauliflower

1/2 cup extra virgin olive oil

2 teaspoons minced onion

1 teaspoon garlic powder

2 teaspoons paprika

1 lemon

Directions:

1. Juice the lemon. Whisk together all the ingredients EXCEPT for the cauliflower in a bowl, and set aside. Preheat the grill to medium heat.

2. Wash the cauliflower, and remove any leaves, slice off the stem so the cauliflower head can stay flat while on the cutting surface. Cut the cauliflower head in half, and make 1-inch-thick slices lengthwise. You will only grill the biggest slices from the center. Place the remaining pieces in a sealable plastic bag, and set aside.

3. Use a brush to coat the steaks with the oil mixture.

4. Place the remaining oil in the bag with the rest of the cauliflower, and shake until well coated.

5. Cook all the cauliflower for about 5 to 7 minutes per side.

6. Serve immediately.

Nutritional Info: Calories: 261 | Sodium: 41 mg | Dietary Fiber: 4.4 g | Total Fat: 25.5 g | Total Carbs: 10.3 g | Protein: 3.1 g.

Grilled Cheese and Tomato Sandwich

Servings: 4 | Prep Time: 5 Minutes | Cook Time: 10 Minutes

This is a simple variation on an American classic. The tomatoes give this easy to make sandwich a nice texture.

Ingredients:

8 slices whole wheat bread

16 slices provolone cheese

4 large tomatoes

Directions:

1. Slice the tomatoes, and preheat the grill to medium heat.

2. Put a slice of cheese on 4 pieces of bread. Then cover the cheese with the tomatoes. Add another slice of cheese on top of the tomatoes. Top with the remaining slices of bread.

3. Grill the sandwiches for 3 to 5 minutes a side.

4. Serve immediately.

Nutritional Info: Calories: 283 | Sodium: 554 mg | Dietary Fiber: 6.0 g |
Total Fat: 10.8 g | Total Carbs: 30.9 g | Protein: 17.0 g.

Grilled Asparagus with Balsamic Soy Butter

Servings: 6 | Prep Time: 5 Minutes | Cook Time: 12 Minutes

The sauce adds tremendous flavor to the asparagus. The balsamic, say sauce, and browned butter compliments the woodsy flavor of the asparagus perfectly.

Ingredients:

2 bunches asparagus

2 teaspoons olive oil

1/8 teaspoon sea salt

Fresh ground black pepper, to taste

2 tablespoons butter

2 teaspoons soy sauce

1 teaspoon balsamic vinegar

Directions:

1. Trim the asparagus. Preheat the grill to medium heat.

2. Mix the asparagus with the olive oil, until the asparagus is well coated, and salt and pepper to taste.

3. Grill the asparagus for 8 to 10 minutes.

4. Place the butter in a small skillet it and melt it. Cook until it starts to brown. Take the butter off the heat, and mix in the vinegar and soy.

5. Top the asparagus with the sauce, and serve.

Nutritional Info: Calories: 57 | Sodium: 167 mg | Dietary Fiber: 0.9 g | Total Fat: 5.5 g | Total Carbs: 1.9 g | Protein: 1.1 g.

Matt Jason

Grilled Corn Fritters

Servings: 6 | Prep Time: 5 Minutes | Cook Time: 10 Minutes

These corn fritters are the perfect appetizer for summer. They have a sweet flavor, and are ready in no time.

Ingredients:

1/3 cup yellow cornmeal
1/4 cup all-purpose flour
1/2 teaspoon baking powder
1/2 teaspoon kosher salt, or more to taste
1/2 teaspoon ground black pepper
Handful of parsley
1/3 cup milk
2 cups grilled corn
Vegetable oil

Directions:

1. Coat the grill with vegetable oil, and preheat to medium heat. Finely chop the parsley.

2. Mix the flour, cornmeal, baking powder, parsley, salt, and pepper with a whisk in a big bowl. Put in the milk, and use a wooden spoon to mix the ingredients together until they become thick. Put in the corn, and mix until the corn is well covered with the cornmeal mixture.

3. Scoop the mixture out with 1/3 cup measuring cup, and place it on the grill. Flatten it out, and cook for about 5 minutes a side, until it becomes brown. Repeat the process until all the corn mixture is used.

4. Serve Immediately.

Nutritional Info: Calories: 94 | Sodium: 206 mg | Dietary Fiber: 2.0 g | Total Fat: 0.9 g | Total Carbs: 20.3 g | Protein: 3.0 g.

Grilled Eggplant with Mustard Vinaigrette

Servings: 4 | Prep Time: 5 Minutes | Cook Time: 10 Minutes

This makes a good side dish or appetizer. The two kinds of mustard in the vinaigrette go well with the simply grilled eggplant.

Ingredients:

    2 medium-sized eggplants, top removed and sliced lengthwise

    Salt and black pepper

    3 tablespoons whole grain mustard

    2 tablespoons white wine vinegar

    1 tablespoon Dijon mustard

    1/2 cup extra virgin olive oil, plus extra for brushing

    1 tablespoon fresh parsley

    1 teaspoon fresh thyme

    1/4 cup micro greens

Directions:

1.	Remove the top from the eggplant, and cut it lengthwise. Chop the parsley and thyme. Preheat the grill to medium-high heat.

2.	Use a brush to coat both sides of the eggplant with olive oil. Salt and pepper to taste.

3.	Mix the mustards, vinegar, and a pinch of salt and pepper using a whisk in a small bowl. Add in the olive oil, and whisk until well mixed. Mix in the parsley and thyme, and add more salt and pepper if necessary.

4.	Place the eggplant on the grille, and grill for 5 minutes. Then flip the eggplant and grill for another 3 minutes. Place the cooked eggplant on a plate.

5.	Top the eggplant with the vinaigrette, and the micro greens. Serve immediately.

Nutritional Info: Calories: 289 | Sodium: 115 mg | Dietary Fiber: 8.8 g |
Total Fat: 26.2 g | Total Carbs: 15.3 g | Protein: 2.8 g.

Matt Jason

Grilled French Fries

Servings: 2-3 | Prep Time: 1 Hour 10 Minutes | Cook Time: 16 Minutes

This is healthy alternative to traditional fries. They won't be as crispy as regular fries, but they're still delicious.

Ingredients:

> 2 – 3 large russet potatoes
>
> 1 tablespoon seasoned salt
>
> 1 tablespoon olive oil

Directions:

1. Slice the potatoes lengthwise into 1/2 to 5/8-inch-thick pieces. Put the pieces into a bowl of cold water for an hour. Towards the end of the hour preheat the grill to medium heat.

2. Place the potatoes in a colander and rinse them off. Pat the potatoes dry.

3. Lightly coat the potatoes with oil, and salt them.

4. Put the potatoes on the grille, and grill them for 3 to 4 minutes a side. Make sure to grill all 4 sides.

Nutritional Info: Calories: 395 | Sodium: 1542 mg | Dietary Fiber: 8.9 g |
Total Fat: 5.0 g | Total Carbs: 58.0 g | Protein: 6.2 g.

Grilled Potatoes with Rosemary and Smoked Paprika

Servings: 6 | Prep Time: 10 Minutes | Cook Time: 40 Minutes

These potatoes smell and taste heavenly thanks to the rosemary, paprika, and onions. The secret is wrapping them in aluminum foil to grill.

Ingredients:

> 1 pound russet potatoes
> 1 medium onion
> 6 garlic cloves
> 1 tablespoon + 1 teaspoon olive oil
> 1 1/2 teaspoons crushed dried rosemary
> 1/2 teaspoon smoked paprika
> 1/2 teaspoon salt
> 1/2 teaspoon ground pepper

Directions:

1. Cut the potatoes in 1-inch pieces and the onion into small chunks. Peel the garlic gloves and cut them into thirds. Preheat the grill to medium heat.

2. Place the potatoes, onions, olive oil, and garlic in a large bowl. Toss until the vegetables are well coated with olive oil. Put in the salt, pepper, rosemary, and paprika, and toss again until the vegetables are well seasoned.

3. Use 2 (24-inch-long) pieces of aluminum foil to create a package for the potato and onions mixture. Make sure all the ends are pinched closed. Cover the package with a 3rd-piece of aluminum foil.

4. Grill the package for 20 minutes and then flip it over and grill for another 15-20 minutes. The potatoes should be brown and tender when finished.

5. The potatoes can stay warm for about 10 minutes in the aluminum foil package if you're not ready to serve immediately.

Nutritional Info: Calories: 93 | Sodium: 200 mg | Dietary Fiber: 2.5 g | Total Fat: 3.3 g | Total Carbs: 15.0 g | Protein: 1.7 g.

Matt Jason

Grilled Romaine with Corn and Avocado

Servings: 2 | Prep Time: 18 Minutes | Cook Time: 12 Minutes

Grilling the romaine gives it the slightest of smoky flavor, but it still stays crisp. The romaine makes the perfect container for the corn and avocado.

Ingredients:

For the Dressing:

2 tablespoons fresh lemon juice

2 tablespoons maple syrup

2 1/2 tablespoons canola or vegetable oil

1 tablespoon mirin (you could also use rice wine vinegar)

1 tablespoon white miso paste

4 garlic cloves

For the Salad:

2 ears of corn

1 avocado

1/4 cup fresh basil leaves

1 head romaine lettuce

Extra-virgin olive oil

Salt and pepper

Directions:

1. Remove the silk, and husk from the corn. Cut the romaine in half lengthwise. Cut the basil into thin ribbons.

2. Place all the dressing ingredients in a food processor, and process until smooth.

3. Preheat the grill to high. Then put the corn on it, and cook the corn, turning so all sides cook evenly for about 5 to 8 minutes. Some of the kernels will blacken. Allow the corn to cool a little bit. Then cut it off the cob, and place it in a bowl.

4. Slice the avocado in half and discard the seed. Remove the flesh from the peel, and cut it into small chunks.

5. Place 1/4 teaspoon salt, 1/4 teaspoon pepper, basil, avocado, and 1 tablespoon dressing into the bowl with the corn. Gently stir until the ingredients are mixed.

6. Lightly coat the cut side of the romaine with about 1 tablespoon olive oil, and salt and pepper to taste.

7. Place the romaine cut side down on the grill, and cook for 1 to 2 minutes, then flip it over and cook for another 1 to 2 minutes.

8. Place the romaine on a serving plate with the cut side up, then add dressing to taste. Place the corn mixture on the romaine. Add more dressing if you'd like, and serve.

Nutritional Info: Calories: 483 | Sodium: 406 mg | Dietary Fiber: 8.6 g | Total Fat: 38.2 g | Total Carbs: 36.5 g | Protein: 4.4 g.

Grilled Sweet Potatoes

Servings: 4 | Prep Time: 20 Minutes | Cook Time: 10 Minutes

This dish seems impossibly simply, but it's delicious in its simplicity. The acid from the limes balances the sweetness of the sweet potato. Feel free to substitute lemons for limes, and parsley or cilantro.

Ingredients:

2 pound sweet potatoes
3 - 4 tablespoons olive oil
Kosher salt

Dressing:

1/4 cup fresh cilantro (including tender stems)
1 teaspoon lime zest or lemon zest
2 tablespoons fresh lime or lemon juice
1/4 cup olive oil
Pinch of salt

Directions:

1. Preheat the grill to high. Cut the sweet potatoes lengthwise into 1/4-inch thick slices. Peel the slices. Brush the sweet potatoes with olive oil and salt to taste. Finely chop the cilantro.

2. Mix all of the dressing ingredients in a bowl.

3. Grill the sweet potatoes for 3 to 6 minutes per side, until they're soft.

4. Toss the cooked sweet potatoes with the dressing. Serve immediately.

Nutritional Info: Calories: 498 | Sodium: 60 mg | Dietary Fiber: 9.4 g | Total Fat: 27 g | Total Carbs: 64 g | Protein: 3.5 g.

Grilled Vegetable Quesadillas with Goat Cheese and Pesto

Servings: 4 | Prep Time: 25 Minutes | Cook Time: 12 Minutes

These quesadillas are filled with grilled vegetables, and melty goat and mozzarella cheese. Grilling the quesadillas adds a delicious smokiness to the tortillas.

Ingredients:

1 small zucchini

1 small summer squash

1 red bell pepper

1 small red onions

1 large Portobello mushroom

2 tablespoons extra virgin olive oil

Salt

White pepper

4 whole grain tortillas

4 tablespoons pesto, divided

2 cups part-skim mozzarella cheese, divided

4-ounce goat cheese, divided

Directions:

1. Clean the mushroom and cut it into 1/2-inch pieces. Cut the onion into 1/4-inch rounds. Diagonally cut the squash and zucchini into 1/4 slices. Remove the stem and seeds from the bell pepper, and quarter it. Preheat the grill to medium heat.

2. Use the olive oil to coat the vegetables, and salt and white pepper to taste.

3. Grill the vegetables for 3 minutes per side, until they become tender. Then allow them to cool for 5 minutes.

4. Slice the vegetables into 1/2-inch pieces.

5. Spread 1 tablespoon of pest on each tortilla, then 1/4 cup mozzarella on half the tortilla, then put in 1/4 cup of the vegetables, and top with 1-ounce. goat cheese. Add another 1/4 cup mozzarella, and fold over one side of the tortilla.

6. Lightly oil the grill, and place the quesadilla on it (the grill should still be at medium heat). Cook the quesadillas for 3 minutes a side. The cheese will be nicely melted when ready.

7. Slice the quesadillas and serve.

Nutritional Info: Calories: 382 | Sodium: 336 mg | Dietary Fiber: 3.8 g |
Total Fat: 27.1 g | Total Carbs: 19.9 g | Protein: 17.2 g.

Grilled Vegetable with Goat Cheese

Servings: 8-10 | Prep Time: 20 Minutes | Cook Time: 20 Minutes

The marinade gives the vegetable a wonderful full flavor. The goat cheese serves as a dip the compliments the vegetables well.

Ingredients:

2 eggplants

1 pound zucchini

1 pound Anaheim green peppers

3 - 4 green bell peppers (or other variety like sweet Italian peppers)

1 pound sweet mini peppers (or other variety like sweet Italian red peppers)

1 pound asparagus

2 - 3 red onions

For the marinade:

1/2 cup olive oil

1/4 cup balsamic vinegar + 1/4 cup apple cider vinegar

4 - 5 garlic cloves

2-3 tablespoons fresh chopped oregano (or 2 tablespoons dry oregano)

Salt to taste

For the whipped goat cheese:

1/2 cup goat cheese

1/4 cup whipping cream

1 clove garlic

Salt to taste

Directions:

1. Slice the zucchini, eggplant, and onions into 1/2-thick pieces. Rinse the peppers. Rinse the asparagus, and slice off the woody bottoms. Smash the garlic. Preheat the grill to medium heat.

2. Season the eggplant with salt and place it in a colander for 20 minutes. Then rinse the eggplant off, and pat it dry.

3. Mix the marinade ingredients together, and use a brush to cover the vegetables..

4. Grill the vegetable for 20 minutes, and flip them over half way through.

5. Place the grilled vegetables on serving plate, and cover them with the remaining marinade.

6. Beat the whipping cream with an electric mixer until soft peaks are created. Put in the remaining goat cheese ingredients, and beat until the mixture is fluffy.

7. Place the goat cheese in a small bowl and serve with the vegetables.

Nutritional Info: Calories: 351 | Sodium: 89 mg | Dietary Fiber: 20.3 g |
Total Fat: 17.2 g | Total Carbs: 48.8 g | Protein: 12.6 g.

Matt Jason

Grilled Zucchini with Lemon Salt

Servings: 8 | Prep Time: 30 Minutes | Cook Time: 20 Minutes

This zucchini recipe pairs well with chicken, fish, and olive oil based pasta. The lemon cuts down the saltiness and brings out the flavor of the zucchini.

Ingredients:

6 whole zucchinis (medium sized)

1/4 cup olive oil

1 teaspoon kosher salt

1 teaspoon black pepper

3 whole lemons

1 teaspoon kosher salt (additional)

Extra olive oil if needed for brushing

Directions:

1. Chop off the tops and bottoms of the zucchini, and cut the zucchini into quarters lengthwise. Zest the lemons. Juice 2 of the lemons.

2. Place the zucchini in an extra-large sealable plastic bag. Add in 1 tablespoon of lemon zest, lemon juice, salt, pepper, and olive oil. Seal the bag and shake it around until the zucchini is well coated. Allow the zucchini to marinate in the bag for 15 to 20 minutes.

3. While the zucchini is marinating preheat the grill to medium-low heat.

4. Grill the zucchini for about 6 minutes a side on all 3 sides. The zucchini will be tender when cooked. Place the cooked zucchini on a serving plate.

5. Take the remaining lemon zest and add 1 tablespoon of kosher salt to it. Chop the mixture together until it's very fine, and becomes lemon salt.

6. Sprinkle the zucchini with the lemon salt and serve.

Nutritional Info: Calories: 87 | Sodium: 597 mg | Dietary Fiber: 2.6 g | Total Fat: 6.7 g | Total Carbs: 8.0 g | Protein: 2.2 g.

Penne with Grilled Vegetable Pesto

Servings: 8 | Prep Time: 5 Minutes | Cook Time: 10 Minutes

This a great dish for a summer night. The pesto and vegetables make a delicious and healthy sauce for the penne.

Ingredients:

2 small summer squash, sliced 1/4-inch-thick

2 small zucchinis, sliced 1/4-in thick

1/2 pound fresh asparagus, trimmed and cut in half widthwise

1 large sweet pepper, sliced 1/4-inch-thick into strips

2 cloves garlic, minced

1/2 cup prepared basil pesto

Salt and pepper to taste

12 ounce cooked penne pasta

Directions:

1. Slice the squash and zucchini 1/4-inch thick slices. Trim the asparagus, and slice them in half widthwise. Mince the garlic. Slice the sweet pepper into 1/4-inch thick pieces. Preheat the grill to medium-high heat.

2. Mix together all the ingredients EXCEPT the penne in a bowl.

3. Place aluminum foil on the grill, and then place the vegetables on the foil. Grill for 8 to 10 minutes, some of the vegetables should have a char on them.

4. Top the cooked pasta with the vegetables, and serve.

Nutritional Info: Calories: 149 | Sodium: 18 mg | Dietary Fiber: 2.0 g | Total Fat: 1.3 g | Total Carbs: 28.9 g | Protein: 6.7 g.

Matt Jason

Foil Packet Grilled Mushrooms

Servings: 4 | Prep Time: 12 Minutes | Cook Time: 25 Minutes

Grilling the mushrooms in foil packets lets them absorb all the flavor from the herbs. It also makes the mushrooms tender and juicy.

Ingredients:

1 pound large mushrooms

2 tablespoons fresh thyme, mint, sage, rosemary or marjoram

2 to 4 garlic cloves

Salt

Freshly ground pepper to taste

2 tablespoons extra virgin olive oil, plus additional for brushing foil

Aluminum foil

Directions:

1. Preheat your grill to medium-high heat. Clean, trim, and slice the mushrooms 1/2-inch thick. Chop the garlic and herbs of your choice. Cut 4 (12x12) pieces of aluminum foil.

2. Mix all the ingredients in a large bowl. Use a brush to coat the dull side of the aluminum foil with olive oil. Place the mushrooms in the middle of the dull side of the aluminum foil. Fold the sides over the mushrooms and seal the edges to make the packets.

3. Grill the packets for 20 to 25 minutes. The mushrooms will be tender when cooked.

4. Put the mushrooms on a plate, and serve.

Nutritional Info: Calories: 106 | Sodium: 11 mg | Dietary Fiber: 3.9 g | Total Fat: 7.6 g | Total Carbs: 9.2 g | Protein: 4.4 g.

Sesame Garlic Grilled Shishido Pepper with Ponzu Aioli

Servings: 2 | Prep Time: 10 Minutes | Cook Time: 4 Minutes

Shishido's have a delicious smoky flavor and can be spicy. The ponzu aioli has a tangy citrusy flavor that compliments the peppers, and helps cut some of the heat.

Ingredients:

14 Shishido peppers
2 teaspoons sesame oil
2 cloves minced garlic
1/4 teaspoon kosher salt
1/4 teaspoon black pepper

Ponzu Aioli:

1/3 cup mayonnaise
2 teaspoons ponzu sauce
1/2 teaspoon sesame oil
1 clove garlic minced
Pinch of kosher salt

Directions:

1. Mince the garlic. Preheat your grill to medium-high heat.

2. Mix all the Shishido ingredients in a bowl, and make sure the peppers are well coated with the other ingredients.

3. Grill the peppers for 2 minutes a side.

4. Put all the ponzu aioli ingredients in a bowl, and use a whisk to combine them.

5. Plate the peppers with a side of the ponzu aioli. Serve immediately.

Nutritional Info: Calories: 237 | Sodium: 765 mg | Dietary Fiber: 2.8 g | Total Fat: 19.1 g | Total Carbs: 17.8 g | Protein: 1.8 g.

CHAPTER

5

Pork/Beef

Bacon Wrapped Asparagus

Servings: 6-8 | Prep Time: 30 Minutes | Cook Time: 15 Minutes

The bacon adds a salty flavor to the earthiness of the asparagus. Make these as an appetizer for your next barbeque.

Ingredients:

1 pound medium asparagus
Extra-virgin olive oil
Freshly ground black pepper
Salt
1 pound hickory smoked bacon
Wooden skewers

Directions:

1. Soak the wooden skewers for 20 minutes in cold water. Trim the bottoms off the asparagus. Preheat your grill to medium-high heat.

2. Put the asparagus on a baking sheet and coat with olive oil. Salt and pepper to taste.

3. Wrap a piece of bacon around 1 piece of asparagus. Use 2 skewers to keep the top and bottom of the bacon in place. Put 3 to 4 pieces of asparagus on each skewer pair.

4. Grill the skewers for 15 minutes, flipping halfway through.

5. Put the asparagus on a serving plate, and discard the skewers. Serve immediately.

Nutritional Info: Calories: 320 | Sodium: 1331 mg | Dietary Fiber: 1.4 g |
Total Fat: 23.8 g | Total Carbs: 3.4 g | Protein: 22.3 g.

Balsamic Grilled Beets

Servings: 4-6 | Prep Time: 1 Hour 5 Minutes | Cook Time: 25 Minutes

The balsamic glaze gives a tangy flavor to these earthy beets. They go great as a side dish, or as a patty for a veggie burger.

Ingredients:

    1/3 cup + 1 tablespoon Balsamic vinegar
    1 clove garlic
    1/2 teaspoon rosemary
    1/4 teaspoon savory
    1/4 teaspoon basil
    1/4 teaspoon sage
    1/4 teaspoon thyme
    1/4 teaspoon marjoram
    4 large beets, sliced into 1/2-inch thick circles

Directions:

1.   Mince the garlic, and cut the beets into 1/2-inch thick circles.

2.   Use a whisk to combine all the Ingredients EXCEPT for the beets in a wide flat dish.

3.   Put the beets in the dish, make sure they're well coated with the mixture, and allow them to rest in it for an hour. Towards the end of the hour preheat the grill to medium-high heat.

4.   Use aluminum foil to completely wrap and seal the beets. Grill them for 20 to 25 minutes. The beets will be soft when ready.

5.   Garnish the beets with a splash of balsamic vinegar, and serve.

Nutritional Info: Calories: 62 | Sodium: 98 mg | Dietary Fiber: 2.7 g | Total Fat: 0.3 g | Total Carbs: 13.2 g | Protein: 2.2 g.

Blackberry Bacon Grilled Cheese Sandwich

Servings: 1 sandwich | Prep Time: 5 Minutes | Cook Time: 10 Minutes

This sandwich is the perfect combination of flavors. It gets sweetness from the blackberry jam, heat from the jalapeno, saltiness from the bacon, and creaminess from the cheese.

Ingredients:

- 1 tablespoon butter
- 2 pieces sourdough bread
- 4 slices swiss cheese
- 4 pieces cooked bacon,
- 1/2 jalapeno (*for less spice, remove seeds)
- 3 tablespoons blackberry jam

Directions:

1. Preheat your grill to medium heat. Slice the jalapeno. Butter 1 side of each piece of bread.

2. Place the cheese, bacon, and jalapeno on the unbuttered side of a piece of bread. Spread the jam on the unbuttered side of the other piece of bread. Then put the sandwich together.

3. Grill the sandwich for about 10 minutes flipping it halfway through. The cheese will be melted, and the bread will be golden when done.

4. Serve immediately.

Nutritional Info: Calories: 599 | Sodium: 843 mg | Dietary Fiber: 2.6 g | Total Fat: 27.6 g | Total Carbs: 61.4 g | Protein: 27.5 g.

Bone-In Ribeye Steak

Servings: 4 | Prep Time: 40 minutes-1 Hour 10 Minutes | Cook Time: 10 minutes

There's not much you need to do to improve the flavor of a good ribeye steak. The butter, and thyme help to bring out the natural flavor of the steak.

Ingredients:

    2 bone-in rib-eye steaks, each 16-ounce and 1 to 1 1/2-inch-thick
    2 tablespoons olive oil
    Kosher salt and freshly ground pepper, to taste
    4 tablespoons (1/2 stick) unsalted butter
    4 fresh thyme sprigs

Directions:

1. Divide the butter into 2 equal portions. Preheat the grill to medium-high heat.

2. Lightly coat the steaks on both sides with olive oil. Put the oiled steaks on a plate, and then cover them with plastic wrap.

3. Allow them to rest for 30 minutes to an hour. Then salt and pepper both sides to taste.

4. Grill the stakes for 5 to 7 minutes, and then flip them over. Place the butter on top of the steaks, and then the thyme.

5. Allow the butter to melt, and baste the steaks with it. Grill for 5 to 7 minutes more if you like your steak medium-rare, continue grilling if you want your steak more done.

6. Place the cooked steaks on a plate, and cover with aluminum foil. The foil should cover the steaks loosely. Let the steaks stand for 5 minutes before serving.

Nutritional Info: Calories: 626 | Sodium: 225 mg | Dietary Fiber: 1.7 g |
Total Fat: 30.2 g | Total Carbs: 3.1 g | Protein: 82.5 g.

Five-Spice Hoisin Kebabs

Servings: 2 | Prep Time: 30 Minutes | Cook Time: 8 Minutes

Five-spice is a mixture of fennel seeds, cloves, star anise, Chinese cinnamon, and Sichuan pepper. It is popular in Chinese cuisine and gives a delicious flavor to these juicy kebabs.

Ingredients:

- 1 (12-ounce) pork tenderloin
- 1/2 teaspoon kosher salt
- 3/4 teaspoons five-spice powder
- 1/2 teaspoon garlic powder
- 1/4 teaspoon cornstarch
- 2 1/2 tablespoons hoisin sauce
- Vegetable oil spray
- 1 scallion

Directions:

1. Trim the fat off the pork, and slice it into 1-inch pieces. Thinly slice the scallions. Preheat your grill to high heat.

2. In a big bowl mix, together the salt and pork, and let it rest for 20 minutes.

3. While the pork is resting, use a whisk to mix together the five-spice powder, cornstarch, and garlic powder. Then mix in the hoisin sauce. Set aside 1 tablespoon of the mixture

4. Mix the larger portion of the five-spice mixture with the pork. Then place the pork on 2 (12-inch) metal skewers, with 1/4-inch of space between pieces of pork. Use the cooking spray to coat the skewers.

5. Brush the grill grates with a little, and grill the skewers for 3 to 4 minutes. Turn them over and brush them with the reserved five-spice mixture. Grill for another 3 to 4 minutes.

6. Place the skewers on a serving platter, and tent the platter with aluminum foil. Allow the skewers to rest for 5 minutes.

7. Top with scallions and serve.

Nutritional Info: Calories: 299 | Sodium: 1003 mg | Dietary Fiber: 1.3 g |
Total Fat: 6.9 g | Total Carbs: 10.4 g | Protein: 45.7 g.

Matt Jason

Grilled Flat-Iron Steak with Chimichurri Sauce

Servings: 2 | Prep Time: 15 Minutes | Cook Time: 8 Minutes

Chimichurri is a sauce and marinade from Argentina that's made with parsley, garlic, and olive oil. It's the perfect pairing for this juicy steak.

Ingredients:

Steak & Dry Rub:

1 pound skirt steak

1 1/2 teaspoons kosher salt

1/3 teaspoon paprika

1-2 tablespoons steak seasoning

1 tablespoon mesquite seasoning (or any other flavor) – optional*

2 tablespoons olive oil

Chimichurri Sauce:

1/2 bunch flat leaf Italian parsley

Green parts of 3-4 green onions

1 teaspoon salt

1-2 cloves garlic

1 tablespoon balsamic vinegar

1/4 cup olive oil

1/2 teaspoon black pepper

Pinch of paprika

1/2 teaspoon red chili flakes (optional – for heat)

Directions:

1. Remove the hard stems from the parsley and roughly chop it. Roughly chop the green onions, discarding the white parts. Preheat the grill to medium-high heat.

2. Use a brush to coat both sides of the steak. Season it with the salt, and spices. Then use your hand to press the seasoning into the steak.

3. Grill the steak for about 5 minutes a side. When you flip, it uses something heavy like a brick wrapped in aluminum foil to flatten the steak.

4. When cooked, put the steak on a warm plate, let it sit for 10 minutes covered with aluminum foil.

5. While the steak is resting, place all the chimichurri ingredients in a blender. Blend until your desired consistency is reached. Salt and pepper to taste if necessary.

6. Slice the steak, and top with the chimichurri. Serve with a side of the chimichurri.

Nutritional Info: Calories: 828 | Sodium: 1355 mg | Dietary Fiber: 2.0 g | Total Fat: 62.4 g | Total Carbs: 5.5 g | Protein: 62.1 g.

Grilled Tahini Pork Skewers

Servings: 4 | Prep Time: 30 Minutes | Cook Time: 6 Minutes

These skewers are full of flavor thanks to the tahini, fish sauce, and lime. They're supremely juicy, and the shiso leaves make a beautiful presentation.

Ingredients:

1/2 cup (140g) tahini

1/2 cup (125ml) coconut milk

2 tablespoons fish sauce

1 tablespoon honey, plus extra to serve

2 tablespoons lime juice

1 tablespoon sesame oil

800g boneless pork neck

1 red bird's-eye chili

1/3 cup (45g) salted peanuts

Micro (baby) purple shiso leaves to serve

Directions:

1. Trim the fat off the pork, and slice it into 1-inch pieces. Thinly slice the chili, and chop the peanuts.

2. Mix the first 6 ingredients in a large bowl.

3. Take out half the mixture and set aside. Mix the pork in the bowl with the other half. Allow the pork to marinate for 15 minutes.

4. Use oil to light grease the grill and preheat it to medium heat.

5. Put the pork on 12 metal skewers, and grill them for 2 to 3 minutes a side. Make sure they're cooked all the way through.

6. Garnish the skewers with the chili, shiso, and honey. Serve with the rest of the tahini on the side.

Nutritional Info: Calories: 655 | Sodium: 857 mg | Dietary Fiber: 5.3 g |
Total Fat: 39.0 g | Total Carbs: 16.9 g | Protein: 62.5 g.

Honey Rosemary Pork Chops

Servings: 4 | Prep Time: 15 Minutes | Cook Time: 14 Minutes

These pork chops have a nice balance of sweet from the honey, and aromatic savory from the rosemary. The pork comes out juicy and tender.

Ingredients:

Vegetable oil, for the grates
1/4 cup honey
4 tablespoons olive oil, divided
2 tablespoons fresh rosemary
4 6-ounce boneless pork chops, each about 3/4-inch thick
Kosher salt and freshly ground black pepper

Directions:

1. Preheat your grill to medium heat, and brush it with a little vegetable oil. Chop the rosemary.

2. Use a whisk to mix the 2 tablespoons olive oil, rosemary, and honey. Divide the glaze into 2 portions, and set aside.

3. Use a brush to lightly coat the pork chops with olive oil, and do the same with half the glaze. Then salt and pepper to taste.

4. Grill the pork chops for 5 to 6 minutes, and then turn them over, and grill for another 6 to 8 minutes. Brush the cooked chops with the rest of the glaze. Let the pork chops sit for 5 minutes, before serving.

Nutritional Info: Calories: 77 | Sodium: 32 mg | Dietary Fiber: 0.9 g | Total Fat: 4.5 g | Total Carbs: 3.6 g | Protein: 5.9 g.

Brined Pork Chops

Servings: 3 | Prep Time: 20 Minutes | Cook time: 4 Minutes

These pork chops cook quickly because they're thinner than the typical pork chop. The brine helps to keep them juicy.

Ingredients:

> 3 pounds thin cut pork chops (1/4" to 1/2" thick, preferably rib chops)
> Brine
> 1/4 cup soy sauce
> 2 tablespoons balsamic vinegar
> 2 tablespoons honey
> 2 tablespoons olive oil

Directions:

1. Use a whisk to combine the brine ingredients in a bowl. Set aside 2 tablespoons of the brine for later.

2. Place the pork chops in a baking dish, and pour in the brine. Make sure both sides of the pork chops are well coated with the brine. Allow the chops to rest for 10 minutes. While the chops are resting preheat the grill to medium heat.

3. Grill the chops for around 2 minutes before rotating 90 degrees. Let the chops cook for another 2 minutes.

4. Top the cooked chops with the reserved brine, and let them sit for 5 minutes before serving.

Nutritional Info: Calories: 1587 | Sodium: 1516 mg | Dietary Fiber: 0 g | Total Fat: 122.1 g | Total Carbs: 13.2 g | Protein: 103.3 g.

Matt Jason

Pineapple Teriyaki Pork Chops

Servings: 4 | Prep Time 2 Hours 10 Minutes | Cook Time: 10 Minutes

These pork chops have a great tropical flavor thanks to the addition of pineapple. The teriyaki sauce helps to balance the flavor of the pineapple.

Ingredients:

1/3 cup orange juice	1/2 teaspoon onion powder
2 tablespoons less-sodium soy sauce	1/2 teaspoon garlic powder
1 tablespoon rice vinegar	4 (4-ounce) boneless pork chops
1 tablespoon brown sugar	2 teaspoons cornstarch
1/2 teaspoon ground ginger	4 thickly sliced fresh pineapple rings

Directions:

1. Trim the fat from the pork chops.
2. Use a whisk to mix together the first 7 ingredients in a bowl.
3. Put the pork chops in a big resealable plastic bag, and put in the marinade. Seal the bag and shake it. Put the bag in the refrigerator for 2 hours, and shake the bag at the hour mark to make sure the chops are evenly coated. Put the chops on a plate, and place the excess marinade in a small saucepan.
4. Put the cornstarch in a bowl with 2 teaspoons of cold water. Allow the cornstarch to dissolve, creating a slurry, and set aside.
5. Heat the marinade on medium heat until it begins to boil. Lower the heat to low, add in the slurry, and use a whisk to mix the ingredients together until the sauce becomes thicker. Take the sauce off the heat, and set aside.
6. Preheat your grill to medium-high heat. Spray the grill light with cooking spray.
7. Grill the pork chops for 4 to 5 minutes, and flip them. Grill for another 4 to 5 minutes. Brush the pork chops with the sauce throughout the grilling process.
8. Grill the pieces of pineapple for 1 to 2 minutes per side.
9. Allow the pork chops to sit for 2 to 4 minutes.
10. Serve the pork chops with a slice of pineapple on top of it.

Nutritional Info: Calories: 197 | Sodium: 517 mg | Dietary Fiber: 0 g | Total Fat: 4.0 g | Total Carbs: 7.5 g | Protein: 30.5 g.

Pork and Pineapple Skewers with Mango Brown Sugar Glaze

Servings: 6 | Prep Time: 8 Hours 20 Minutes | Cook Time: 20 Minutes

These skewers are truly a tropical delight. The mango glaze gives the pork a sweet flavor that pairs well with the pineapple. Make sure you plan and marinate the pork overnight.

Ingredients:

1 1/2 pounds country pork ribs	1/4 cup balsamic vinegar
8 ounces can, crushed pineapple (do not drain)	1 pineapple
1/2 cup brown sugar	2 mangos

Mango Brown Sugar Glaze:

1 mango	1/2 cup brown sugar
1/2 cup water	1/2 teaspoon ground ginger

Directions:

1. Cut the pork into 1 inch pieces.

2. Place the pork, canned pineapple, vinegar, and brown sugar in a large resealable plastic bag. Allow the mixture to marinate for at least 8 hours.

3. Once the mixture is ready, core, and cut the pineapple into chunks. Peel, and cut the mango into chunks. Place the fruit, and pork onto 6 skewers, alternating between pieces of fruit and pork.

4. Slice the mango for the glaze into small chunks. Place the mango and 1/2 cup water in a blender and puree it. Once pureed, place it in a saucepan with the brown sugar on high heat.

5. When it starts to boil, lower the heat to low for about 5 to 7 minutes. Mix in the ginger and take the saucepan off the heat. Preheat your grill to medium-high heat.

6. Place the skewers on the grill, and brush them with the glaze throughout the cooking process. Grill the skewers for around 10 minutes a side.

7. Serve immediately.

Nutritional Info: Calories: 453 | Sodium: 75 mg | Dietary Fiber: 1.3 g |
Total Fat: 20.2 g | Total Carbs: 36.4 g | Protein: 30.5 g.

Pork Balls on a Stick

Servings: 4 | Prep Time: 15 Minutes | Cook Time: 15 Minutes

This bacon-wrapped pork skewers are filled with a delicious surprise. They're filled with cream cheese, and chives.

Ingredients:

2 pound pork tenderloin

2 cups cream cheese

1/2 cup chives

Dash sugar (no more than a teaspoon)

16 slices bacon

1/2 cup soy sauce

Directions:

1. Preheat the grill to medium-high heat. Combine the chives, sugar, and cream cheese with a spatula.

2. Slice up the pork into 2-ounce slices.

3. Flatten the pork with a meat mallet.

4. Cover one side of the pork with the cream cheese mixture, and roll it up.

5. Take a piece of bacon and wrap it around the pork.

6. Put 4 pork balls on each skewer, and cover them with soy sauce.

7. Grill the pork for 10 to 15 minutes, flipping halfway through the grilling process.

Nutritional Info: Calories: 878 | Sodium: 2824 mg | Dietary Fiber: 0 g |
Total Fat: 58.5 g | Total Carbs: 6.2 g | Protein: 79.2 g.

Pork Saltimbocca

Servings: 4 | Prep Time: 5 Minutes | Cook Time: 15 Minutes

Saltimbocca is an Italian dish that traditionally uses veal instead of pork. It's a delish mix of salty and tangy.

Ingredients:

- 4 boneless pork chops, each 3/4 to 1-inch-thick and 6 to 7 ounce.
- Kosher salt and freshly ground pepper, to taste
- 8 fresh sage leaves
- 8 thin prosciutto slices
- Olive oil for brushing
- Balsamic vinegar for drizzling

Directions:

1. Preheat your grill to medium-high heat. Warm a plate.

2. Salt and pepper both sides of the pork chops to taste. Place 2 sage leaves on top of each pork chop, and then wrap them with 2 pieces of prosciutto. Brush both sides of the pork chops with oil lightly.

3. Grill the pork chops for 6 to 7 minutes a side. The chops are done when a meat thermometer stuck in the center of the chops reads 140F. Put the cooked pork chops on the warmed plate.

4. Use aluminum foil to lightly cover the chops and let them sit for 10 minutes. Top the chops with a little balsamic vinegar, and serve.

Nutritional Info: Calories: 320 | Sodium: 642 mg | Dietary Fiber: 1.9 g |
Total Fat: 8.8 g | Total Carbs: 3.9 g | Protein: 53.9 g.

Pork Souvlaki with Lemon Rice

Servings: 6 Skewers | Prep Time: 2 Hours 30 Minutes | Cook Time: 40 Minutes

This is a simple Greek dish where the pork is marinated in olive oil, lemon, and oregano. It gives the pork a delicious tangy flavor.

Ingredients:

2 pounds pork tenderloin

3 Meyer lemons or 4 regular lemons

1/2 cup fruity olive oil

6 large cloves of garlic

3 tablespoons oregano

3 teaspoons kosher salt, divided

1 teaspoon freshly ground black pepper

1 cup white rice

1 tablespoon butter

2 tablespoons Italian parsley

Directions:

1. Zest the lemons. Mince the garlic. Mince the parsley. Trim off the fat from the pork, and slice it into 1 inch pieces. Put the pork in a large resealable plastic bag.

2. Combine the juice of 3 regular lemons, or 2 Meyer lemons with the olive oil in a bowl. Mix in the oregano, salt, Pepper, and garlic. Place the mixture in the plastic bag with the pork, and make sure the pork is well coated. Refrigerate the pork for at least 2 hours or up to 24 hours. The longer it marinates the better it will taste.

3. Preheat the grill to medium-high heat. Place the pork on either metal or wood skewers. If using wood skewers soak them in water for 20 minutes before using.

4. While grill is preheating, place the rice, 2 cups water, the juice from the remaining lemon, lemon zest, 1 teaspoon salt, and butter in a saucepan. Allow the mixture to come to a boil on high heat. Then lower the heat and allow the rice to simmer covered for 20 minutes. Once the rice has cooked, let it rest for 10 minutes. Then salt and pepper to taste, use a fork to fluff it and mix in 1 tablespoon parsley.

5. When the rice is cooking, Cook the skewers for 10 to 15 minutes. Rotate the skewers throughout the cooking process to make sure the cook evenly. Once cooked, put the skewers on a plate, and cover the plate with aluminum foil for 5 minutes.

6. Top the skewers with a little lemon juice, and remaining parsley. Serve on top of the rice.

Nutritional Info: Calories: 519 | Sodium: 1267 mg | Dietary Fiber: 3.1 g |
Total Fat: 24.7 g | Total Carbs: 32.7 g | Protein: 42.9 g.

Grilled Brown Sugar Chili Pork Tenderloin

Servings: 4 | Prep Time: 5 Minutes | Cook Time: 20 Minutes

This dish is both sweet from the brown sugar, and savory from the paprika, and chili powder. Try serving it with a baked potato, or baked sweet potato.

Ingredients:

1 tablespoon chili powder

1 tablespoon brown sugar

1 teaspoon smoked paprika

1/8 teaspoon ground cinnamon

1 pork tenderloin

1 tablespoon grape seed oil

Directions:

1. Preheat your grill to medium heat. Clean and dry the pork.

2. Mix all the ingredients EXCEPT for the pork, and oil in a bowl.

3. Cover the pork with the grapeseed oil. Then season both sides of the pork with the rub. Grill the pork for 10 minutes, and then flip it over and grill it for another 10 minutes. The center of the pork will be 160F when it's ready.

4. Serve immediately, sliced.

Nutritional Info: Calories: 77 | Sodium: 32 mg | Dietary Fiber: 0.9 g |
Total Fat: 4.5 g | Total Carbs: 3.6 g | Protein: 5.9 g.

Sausage and Vegetable Foil Packets

Servings: 4 | Prep Time: 10 Minutes | Cook Time: 20 Minutes

Cooking all the ingredients together allows the flavors to mix. The Cajun flavor makes everything delicious.

Ingredients:

1 (12.8 ounce) package smoked andouille sausage

1 pound baby red potatoes

1 pound green beans

8 ounce cremini mushrooms

1 onion

4 tablespoons unsalted butter

4 teaspoons Cajun seasoning

Kosher salt and freshly ground black pepper to taste

2 tablespoons fresh parsley leaves

Directions:

1. Thinly slice the sausage. Quarter the potatoes, and halve the mushrooms. Chop the onion, and parsley. Preheat your grill to high heat.

2. Rip out 4, 12-inch-long sheets of aluminum foil. Divide all the ingredients into 4 equal portions. Put the vegetables, and sausage in the middle of each piece of aluminum foil.

3. Turn up the sides of the aluminum packets. Add in the seasoning and butter, and toss all ingredients together. Fold of the sides of the aluminum foil, and seal the packets.

4. Grill the packets for 12 to 15 minutes. Garnish with parsley, and serve.

Nutritional Info: Calories: 559 | Sodium: 1285 mg | Dietary Fiber: 7.2 g |
Total Fat: 36.8 g | Total Carbs: 35.8 g | Protein: 23.6 g.

Steak Skewers with Mushrooms and Potatoes

Servings: 6 | Prep Time: 2 Hours 15 Minutes | Cook Time: 15 Minutes

These skewers are simply marinated with oil, balsamic and spices. The marinade really brings out the flavor of the steak.

Ingredients:

- 1 pound steak
- 8 ounces mushrooms
- 1 pound small potatoes
- 1/4 cup olive oil
- 1/4 cup balsamic vinegar
- 3 cloves garlic, minced
- 1 teaspoon salt
- 1/2 teaspoon pepper
- 1/2 teaspoon dried rosemary
- 1/2 teaspoon dried oregano

Directions:

1. Wash and dry the mushrooms. Slice the steak into 1 inch pieces. Place both the steak and mushrooms on a rimmed baking sheet.

2. Use a whisk to mix together the remaining ingredients EXCEPT for the potatoes in a bowl. Cover the mushrooms and steak with the marinade, and let rest in the refrigerator for 2 hours covered.

3. While marinating, place the potatoes in a big pot of salted water, and bring them to a boil. Cook the potatoes for 8 to 10 minutes. They will be slightly tender when ready. Allow the potatoes to cool a little.

4. Preheat the grill to medium-high heat. Place the steak, potatoes, and mushrooms on skewers.

5. Grill the skewers for 5 to 6 minutes a side. When the skewers are done, salt and pepper to taste.

6. Serve immediately.

Nutritional Info: Calories: 288 | Sodium: 429 mg | Dietary Fiber: 2.4 g | Total Fat: 12.4 g | Total Carbs: 14.0 g | Protein: 29.9 g.

Teriyaki Beef Skewers

Servings: 4 | Prep Time: 40 Minutes | Cook Time: 10 Minutes

These skewers are easy to make, and delicious. The teriyaki compliments the rich flavor of the beef perfectly.

Ingredients:

1 pound beef strips, stir-fry style (or cut your own from a strip steak)

1/4 cup soy sauce

2 tablespoons brown sugar

1 tablespoon rice vinegar

1 clove garlic

1/4 teaspoon onion powder

1/4 teaspoon ginger powder (or 1 teaspoon of minced fresh ginger)

Enough skewers for all the meat

Directions:

1. Soak wooden skewers in water for at least 20 minutes. Mince the garlic.

2. In a bowl, use a whisk to mix together all the ingredients except for the beef.

3. Allow the beef to marinate in the sauce for at least 30 minutes. Toward the end of the marinating process preheat the grill to medium-high heat.

4. Place the beef on the skewers.

5. Grill the skewers for about 2 to 3 minutes a side.

6. Serve immediately.

Nutritional Info: Calories: 241 | Sodium: 975 mg | Dietary Fiber: 0 g | Total Fat: 7.1 g | Total Carbs: 6.1 g | Protein: 35.5 g.

Vietnamese Lemongrass Pork

Servings: 4 | Prep Time: 1 hour 20 Minutes | Cook Time: 8 Minutes

This dish is incredibly fragrant, and citrusy thanks to the lemongrass. It pairs well with rice or serve it with cold rice noodles, and some vegetables as a salad.

Ingredients:

1 pound boneless pork shoulder steak, about 1/2-inch thick

Marinade:

1 1/2 to 2 tablespoons granulated or light brown sugar

1 tablespoon garlic

1 tablespoon shallot or yellow onion

1 stalk lemongrass

1/4 teaspoon black pepper

1 1/2 teaspoons dark (black) soy sauce

1 1/2 tablespoons fish sauce

1 tablespoon oil

Directions:

1. Trim the lemongrass, and roughly chop it. Slice the pork shoulder into 3-4-inch-long pieces. Roughly chop the garlic, and shallot.

2. Place all the ingredients EXCEPT for the pork in a food processor. Pulse until the mixture becomes smooth.

3. Place the marinade in a bowl with the pork. Make sure the pork is well coated with the marinade. Cover, and let rest for an hour. Towards the end of the marinating process preheat your grill to medium-high heat.

4. Grill the pork for 6 to 8 minutes flipping throughout. Make sure the pork is completely cooked.

5. Let pork sit for 10 minutes, covered before serving.

Nutritional Info: Calories: 220 | Sodium: 700 mg | Dietary Fiber: 0 g | Total Fat: 7.4 g | Total Carbs: 6.6 g | Protein: 30.4 g.

CHAPTER
6

Chicken,
Duck and Turkey

Barbeque Chicken, Zucchini, Corn, and Quinoa Salad

Servings: 4 | Prep Time: 10 Minutes | Cook Time: 20 Minutes

This is a great combination of summer flavors. The quinoa gives this salad a light and nutritious base.

Ingredients:

4 cup Quinoa

1 pound boneless skinless chicken breasts or thighs

Salt and pepper to taste

1/2 cup BBQ sauce

1 pound zucchini

2 ears corn

1/4 cup crumbled feta

1/4 cup green onions

2 tablespoons cilantro

1/4 cup BBQ sauce

Directions:

1. Quarter the zucchini lengthwise. Chop the cilantro. Preheat the grill to medium-high heat.

2. Salt and pepper the chicken to taste. Grill the chicken for 4 to 6 minutes a side. Then brush it with the barbeque sauce, and let it rest for a few minutes. Then cut it up.

3. Grill the zucchini and corn for 4 to 6 minutes, flipping halfway through. When cooked, cut the corn from the cob.

4. Place all the ingredients in a bowl, and mix them together. Add a little barbeque sauce to taste, and serve.

Nutritional Info: Calories: 238 | Sodium: 854 mg | Dietary Fiber: 0 g |
Total Fat: 4.7 g | Total Carbs: 28.9 g | Protein: 20.1 g.

Barbeque Spiced Grilled Turkey

Servings: 12 | Prep Time: 10 Hours+ | Cook Time: 1 Hour

This is a great recipe if you want a nontraditional Thanksgiving turkey. The best part is it only takes an hour to cook.

Ingredients:

- 2 tablespoons hot smoked paprika
- 1 tablespoon dried savory
- 1 tablespoon ground cumin
- 1 tablespoon mustard powder
- 1 teaspoon cayenne pepper
- 1/4 cup (packed) plus 3 tablespoons light brown sugar
- 1/2 cup kosher salt
- 1 (12–14 pounds) turkey (backbone removed, breastbone split)
- Vegetable oil (for grill)

Directions:

1. Halve the turkey.
2. Mix together the first 6 ingredients EXCEPT for the 3 tablespoons of brown sugar. Put 3 tablespoons of the mixture into a bowl, and mix with the salt. Put the large amount of spice mixture away. Use the rub/salt mixture to completely cover the turkey. Refrigerate the turkey, uncovered, for 8 to 12 hours.
3. Rinse off the turkey, and pat it dry. Use the reserved spice mixture to completely cover the turkey, and let it rest for 2 hours so that the turkey is room temperature.
4. Towards the end of the resting period, preheat the grill to medium-high heat, and lightly grease it.
5. Put the turkey on the grill skin side up with the legs closest to direct heat. Make sure the breasts are facing each other.
6. Put an oven thermometer in the indirect cooking area, and cover it. Let the turkey cook for 20 minutes before moving the turkey so that the neck is closest to the direct heat zone. Look at the thermometer, and make sure it says 325F. Adjust if it doesn't.
7. Cook for 20 more minutes, and then check to see how cooked the turkey is. Do the same thing every 10 minutes until the turkey is done.
8. Place the turkey on a serving plate, and allow it to rest for 30 minutes before serving.

Nutritional Info: Calories: 931 | Sodium: 1590 mg | Dietary Fiber: 0.8 g |
Total Fat: 27.0 g | Total Carbs: 6.7 g | Protein: 155.5 g

Matt Jason

Chicken Avocado Burgers

Servings: 4 | Prep Time: 7 Minutes | Cook Time: 12 Minutes

These make a great alternative to traditional hamburgers. The avocados make these burgers creamy and delicious.

Ingredients:

- 1 pound ground chicken
- 1 large ripe avocado
- 1 clove of garlic
- 1/3 cup panko crumbs or almond meal (for Paleo eaters)
- 1 poblano or jalapeño pepper (optional)
- 1/2 teaspoon salt
- 1/4 teaspoon pepper

Directions:

1. Preheat the grill to medium heat. Chop the garlic. Cut the avocado into chunks. Mince the poblano or jalapeno. Mix all the ingredients in a bowl.

2. Form the mixture into 4 equal patties.

3. Grill the patties for 5 to 6 minutes a side.

4. Serve with your favorite condiments.

Nutritional Info: Calories: 355 | Sodium: 457 mg | Dietary Fiber: 3.8 g | Total Fat: 18.7 g | Total Carbs: 11.1 g | Protein: 35.0 g.

Buffalo Chicken Grilled Cheese Sandwich

Servings: 4 | Prep Time: 10 Minutes | Cook Time: 10 Minutes

Here's two classic dishes combined in one easy dish. The buffalo chicken gives a huge amount of flavor to this grilled cheese.

Ingredients:

2 cooked and shredded large boneless skinless chicken breasts

1/3 cup buffalo sauce

8 slices cheddar cheese

8 slices bread

2-3 tablespoons butter or a non-dairy butter spread

Directions:

1. Set the butter out so that it's room temperature. Preheat your grill to medium heat.

2. Mix the chicken and buffalo sauce in a bowl, until the chicken is well coated.

3. Butter one side of each piece of bread.

4. Put 1/4 of the chicken on the unbuttered side of 4 slices of bread.

5. Put 2 pieces of cheese on the chicken, and top with the unbuttered side of the remaining pieces of bread.

6. Grill the sandwiches for 4 to 5 minutes a side. The bread should be golden brown on both sides, and the cheese melted when done.

7. Serve immediately.

Nutritional Info: Calories: 470 | Sodium: 570 mg | Dietary Fiber: 0 g |
Total Fat: 30.2 g | Total Carbs: 9.8 g | Protein: 35.9 g.

Matt Jason

Caprese Stuffed Chicken

Servings: 4 | Prep Time: 10 Minutes | Cook Time: 13 Minutes

The chicken is stuffed with mozzarella, and tomatoes making every bite a mouth full of flavor. The balsamic gives this dish a nice sweet, and saltiness.

Ingredients:

- 1 pound skinless boneless chicken breast
- 1/4 teaspoon black pepper
- 1/4 cup cherry tomatoes, or 1 plum tomato
- 5 basil leaves
- 1/2 cup mozzarella cheese
- 1/4 cup balsamic dressing
- Balsamic glaze (optional)

Directions:

1. Slice the tomatoes thinly. Dice the basil leaves. Preheat your grill to medium-low heat. Slice a slit into the center of the chicken, but make sure not to cut all the way through.

2. Pepper the inside of the slit to taste. Then place an even amount of cheese, and tomatoes inside the chicken breasts.

3. Use a brush to coat one side of the chicken with the dressing. Put that side down on the grill for 7 minutes. Brush the top side of the chicken with the dressing. Flip after the 7 minutes, and grill for another 5 minutes. Make sure chicken is completely cooked through.

4. Top with basil and balsamic glaze if desired. Serve immediately.

Nutritional Info: Calories: 209 | Sodium: 367 mg | Dietary Fiber: 0 g |
Total Fat: 4.8 g | Total Carbs: 2.5 g | Protein: 37.8 g.

Grilled Chicken Caesar Wrap

Servings: 4 | Prep Time: 12 Minutes | Cook Time: 13 Minutes

These chicken wraps are more flavorful than the average chicken wrap because both the chicken, and romaine are grilled. These wraps are easy to make, and are great for lunch, or dinner.

Ingredients:

3 tablespoons lemon juice

2 tablespoons extra-virgin olive oil

2 tablespoons low-fat mayonnaise

1 clove garlic

1/2 teaspoon freshly ground pepper

2 boneless skinless chicken breasts (about 1-pound total)

1/8 teaspoon salt

2 small romaine hearts

1/3 cup shredded parmesan cheese

4 (8 to 9-inch) spinach wraps

Directions:

1. Preheat your grill to medium-high heat, and oil it. Mince the garlic. Trim the chicken. Slice the romaine in half longwise.

2. Mix together the mayonnaise, olive oil, garlic, lemon juice, and pepper.

3. Grill the chicken for about 12 minutes, flipping halfway through. Grill the romaine during the last two minutes of grilling. Make sure to flip them once.

4. Slice the chicken into small pieces. Slice off the bottoms off the romaine. Add the chicken, cheese, and romaine to the Caesar dressing. Mix everything together. Place the wraps on the grill for 1 minute to warm them. Divide the mixture among the 4 wraps, roll them up, and serve.

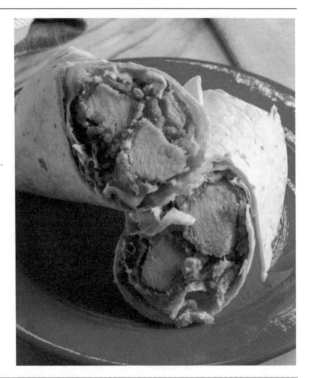

Nutritional Info: Calories: 325 | Sodium: 269 mg | Dietary Fiber: 0 g | Total Fat: 18.9 g | Total Carbs: 3.0 g | Protein: 34.7 g.

Matt Jason

Chicken Fajita Salad

Servings: 4 | Prep Time: 2 Hours 20 Minutes | Cook Time: 12 Minutes

This dish takes all the delicious grilled flavor of fajitas, and makes them into a healthy salad. The marinade does double duty as the dressing, which saves time.

Ingredients:

Marinade/Dressing:

3 tablespoons olive oil	1 teaspoon brown sugar
100ml (just over 1/3 cup) freshly squeezed lime juice	3/4 teaspoon red chili flakes (adjust to your preference of spice)
2 tablespoons fresh chopped cilantro	1/2 teaspoon ground cumin
2 cloves garlic	1 teaspoon salt

Salad:

4 boneless skinless chicken thigh fillets	5 cups romaine (or cos) lettuce leaves
1/2 yellow bell pepper	2 avocados, sliced
1/2 red bell pepper	Extra cilantro leaves to garnish
1/2 onion	Sour cream (optional) to serve

Directions:

1. Deseed and slice the bell peppers. Slice the onion. Wash and dry the romaine. Crush the garlic. Chop the cilantro for the marinade.

2. Use a whisk to mix together the marinade ingredients. Set aside half of it in the refrigerator for the dressing. Place the other half in a bowl with the chicken. Make sure the chicken is well coated with the marinade. Let the chicken marinate for 2 hours. Towards the end of the 2 hours preheat the grill to medium-high heat.

3. Grill the chicken until it's crispy on both sides, and golden in color. Make sure the chicken is completely cooked.

4. Cut the chicken into desired sized pieces. Mix the chicken with the other salad ingredients, and top with the set aside marinade. Toss the salad, and serve.

Nutritional Info: Calories: 485 | Sodium: 665 mg | Dietary Fiber: 7.9 g |
Total Fat: 36.6 g | Total Carbs: 15.2 g | Protein: 27.3 g

Cilantro Lime Grilled Chicken with Strawberry Salsa

Servings: 4 | Prep Time: 50 Minutes | Cook Time: 10 Minutes

This is the perfect dish for summer. It combines the fresh flavors, of cilantro, lime, and strawberry to make a light, refreshing dish.

Ingredients:

For the strawberry salsa:

1 pound strawberries	1 lime
1/4 cup red or green onion	2 tablespoons cilantro
1 jalapeno	Salt to taste

For the Cilantro Lime Grilled Chicken:

1 pound boneless and skinless chicken breasts	2 tablespoons cilantro
1/4 cup lime juice	1 clove garlic
1 tablespoon oil	1 jalapeno (optional)
	Salt and pepper to taste

Directions:

1. Grate the garlic, chop the cilantro, and finely dice the jalapeno if using.

2. Mix together all the chicken ingredients EXCEPT for the chicken. Place the marinade and chicken in a bowl, and let it rest for at 30 Minutes. Refrigerate, covered, if marinating long.

3. While the chicken is marinating, dice the strawberries, finely dice the onions and jalapeno, zest and juice the lime, and chop the cilantro. Combine the ingredients together, and salt and pepper to taste. Then preheat the grill to medium-high heat.

4. Cook the chicken for 3 to 5 minutes a side.

5. Use the salsa to top the chicken, and serve immediately.

Nutritional Info: Calories: 292 | Sodium: 139 mg | Dietary Fiber: 3.0 g |
Total Fat: 12.2 g | Total Carbs: 11.6 g | Protein: 33.9 g.

Grilled Chicken Cordon Bleu

Servings: 4 | Prep Time: 2-4 Hours | Cook Time: 16 Minutes

This delicious chicken dish is topped with ham, and Swiss cheese. It's marinated simply in a sauce highlighted by Dijon, and honey.

Ingredients:

5 tablespoons Dijon mustard

3 tablespoons honey

2 teaspoons soy sauce

1 teaspoon lemon juice

3 tablespoons mayonnaise

4 boneless skinless chicken breasts

4 slices deli ham

4 ounce swiss cheese

Directions:

1. Mix the first 4 ingredients together in a bowl. Set aside 3 tablespoons of the marinade.

2. Place the remaining marinade in a large resealable plastic bag with the chicken, and refrigerate it for 2 to 4 hours.

3. Combine the set aside marinade with the mayonnaise, and refrigerate it.

4. When you're about ready to cook the chicken, preheat your grill to medium heat.

5. Cook the chicken for 12 to 14 minutes, flipping the chicken halfway through.

6. Top the chicken with cheese and ham, and grill for another minute or 2, until the cheese is melted.

7. Serve with the sauce on the side.

Nutritional Info: Calories: 536 | Sodium: 995 mg | Dietary Fiber: 1.1 g |
Total Fat: 25.6 g | Total Carbs: 19.5 g | Protein: 55.7 g.

Duck Poppers

Servings: 4 | Prep Time: 3 Hours 20 Minutes | Cook Time: 10 Minutes

This is a great dish for both duck fans, and people that don't like it. The cheese, jalapeno, and bacon give a world of flavor that balances the flavor of the duck.

Ingredients:

4 duck breast halves

1 regular brick of cream cheese

1 jar mild, medium, or hot jalapeno pepper slices

1 package of thick cut, uncooked bacon

1 bottle of Italian dressing

1 box of wooden toothpicks

Directions:

1. Remove the bones and skin from the duck.

2. Put the duck in a large resealable plastic bag with the dressing. Make sure the duck is well coated with the dressing, and refrigerate it for 3 hours.

3. Preheat the grill to medium-high heat. Use a knife to butterfly the chicken. Make sure not to cut all the way through.

4. Put as many jalapenos as you would like, and a piece of cream cheese in the middle of the butterflied duck, and then fold half of the breast over it. Wrap a piece of bacon around each breast. Use toothpicks to make sure the breast doesn't open.

5. Grill the duck for 10 minutes, flipping halfway through. You can grill longer if you don't like you duck medium rare.

6. Serve immediately.

Nutritional Info: Calories: 307 | Sodium: 149 mg | Dietary Fiber: 0 g |
Total Fat: 24.4 g | Total Carbs: 7.0 g | Protein: 15.1 g

Matt Jason

Foil Grilled Chicken and Vegetables

Servings: 4 | Prep Time: 10 Minutes | Cook Time: 25 Minutes

All the flavors come together when they're grilled in an aluminum foil packet. Use your favorite barbeque sauce gives the chicken a delicious flavor.

Ingredients:

8 aluminum foil sheets large enough to wrap around one chicken breast

4 (4-ounce each) boneless skinless chicken breasts

1/2-cup barbecue sauce

1 zucchini

1 red, green, or yellow bell pepper

8 asparagus spears

Salt and fresh ground pepper to taste

Extra virgin olive oil

Directions

1. Slice the bell pepper into thin strips. Cut the zucchini into thin rounds.

2. Stack 2 pieces of aluminum foil on top of each other, and do the same until you have 4 stacks.

3. Put the chicken in each stack, and salt and pepper to taste. Then use a brush to coat the chicken with 1 to 2 tablespoons of barbeque sauce.

4. Divide the vegetables equally amongst the stacks. Salt and pepper the vegetable to taste.

5. Top everything with a small amount of olive oil.

6. Fold up the sides of the stack over the chicken, and seal the packets shut.

7. Grill the packets for 20 to 25 minutes flipping once, until chicken is cooked through.

8. Allow the chicken to sit for a couple minutes before serving.

Nutritional Info: Calories: 307 | Sodium: 457 mg | Dietary Fiber: 3.6 g |
Total Fat: 8.9 g | Total Carbs: 20.2 g | Protein: 35.3 g.

Grilled Chicken Parmesan

Servings: 4 | Prep Time: 10 Minutes | Cook Time: 15 Minutes

Grilling the chicken instead of breading and frying it makes this dish healthier. Grilling also gives this dish a nice smoky flavor.

Ingredients:

> **4 boneless skinless chicken breasts**
> **1 jar of pasta sauce**
> **2/3 cups shredded parmesan cheese**

Directions:

1. Preheat the grill to medium-high heat.

2. Grill the chicken for about 10 minutes, flipping halfway through.

3. Set your broiler to high.

4. When chicken is done, place it on a baking sheet lined with parchment paper, or a non-stick baking sheet. Place 1 tablespoon of pasta sauce on top of the chicken, and then 1 tablespoon of parmesan cheese.

5. Broil the chicken until the cheese melts, about 4 minutes.

6. Serve immediately.

Nutritional Info: Calories: 285 | Sodium: 398 mg | Dietary Fiber: 1.6 g |
Total Fat: 11.1 g | Total Carbs: 8.8 g | Protein: 35.5 g.

Matt Jason

Grilled Chicken Italiano

Servings: 4 | Prep Time: 12 Minutes | Cook Time: 13 Minutes

This dish puts all of the ingredients in the middle of the chicken instead of topping it. The dressing gives it a nice Italian flavor.

Ingredients:

 4 (4 ounces) chicken breasts
 4 roasted red pepper strips
 Approximately 20 baby spinach leaves
 4 string cheese
 Italian dressing for basting

Directions:

1. Use a knife to butterfly the chicken. Preheat your grill to medium-high heat.

2. Divide the spinach leaves amongst the chicken, and put them in the middle.

3. Top the spinach with the string cheese, and the peppers.

4. Roll the chicken up, and use a couple toothpicks to secure the ends.

5. Grill the chicken for 10 minutes, flipping halfway through. Grill longer if necessary.

6. Serve immediately.

Nutritional Info: Calories: 171 | Sodium: 174 mg | Dietary Fiber: 3.6 g | Total Fat: 8.3 g | Total Carbs: 9.2 g | Protein: 15.0 g.

Grilled Chicken Nuggets

Servings: 30 Nuggets | Prep Time: 40 Minutes | Cook Time: 10 Minutes

These are a healthier version of everyone's favorite bite sized dish. The pickle juicy works as a brine to keep the nuggets juicy.

Ingredients:

1 pound boneless skinless chicken breasts

1/2 cup dill pickle juice

1/4 cup milk

2 teaspoons powdered sugar

1 1/2 teaspoons kosher salt

1 teaspoon black pepper

1/4 teaspoon garlic powder

1/4 teaspoon paprika

1/4 celery salt

Honey Mustard Dipping Sauce:

1/3 cup mayonnaise

1 tablespoon honey

2 teaspoons Dijon mustard

1 teaspoon yellow mustard

1 teaspoon apple cider vinegar

1/4 teaspoon kosher salt

Directions:

1. Slice the chicken into bite sized chunks. In a bowl, combine it with the milk, and pickle juice. Allow it sit for 30 minutes.

2. While the chicken is marinating, mix all the honey mustard ingredients, and place it in the refrigerator until ready to serve.

3. Pat the chicken dry.

4. Combine the spices in a bowl, and toss the chicken with it. Preheat the grill to high heat.

5. Grill the chicken for 3 minutes a side. Make sure the chicken is cooked through.

6. Serve immediately with the sauce.

Nutritional Info: Calories: 43 | Sodium: 174 mg | Dietary Fiber: 0 g | Total Fat: 2.0 g | Total Carbs: 1.6 g | Protein: 4.5 g.

Grilled Chicken Spinach Salad with Dried Cranberries

Servings: 4 | Prep Time: 20 Minutes | Cook Time: 12 Minutes

This salad is quick and easy to make. It has both a sweet and savory taste.

Ingredients:

4 (6-ounce) skinless boneless chicken breast halves

1 tablespoon olive oil

1/2 teaspoon salt

1/2 teaspoon freshly ground black pepper

Cooking spray

1/3 cup celery

1/3 cup sweetened dried cranberries

1/4 cup toasted pecans

3 green onions

3 tablespoons light sour cream

3 tablespoons canola mayonnaise

2 teaspoons fresh lemon juice

Directions:

1. Finely chop the celery. Chop the pecans. Thinly slice the onions. Preheat your grill to medium-high heat and grease it with cooking spray.

2. Use a brush to coat both sides of the chicken with oil. Salt and pepper to taste. Grill the chicken for about 12 minutes, flipping halfway through. Let the chicken sit for 10 minutes, and then slice it.

3. While the chicken is resting, Mix the remaining ingredients together. Then mix with chicken. Plate and serve.

Nutritional Info: Calories: 384 | Sodium: 580 mg | Dietary Fiber: 0.9 g |
Total Fat: 15.2 g | Total Carbs: 5.4 g | Protein: 55.4 g.

Grilled Chicken Stuffed with Peppers and Cheese

Servings: 4 | Prep Time: 10 Minutes | Cook Time: 20 Minutes

Stuffing the chicken gives you maximum flavor with each bite. The sweet peppers and jack cheese give this dish a ton of flavor.

Ingredients:

4 boneless skinless chicken breast

8 sweet peppers

4 slices pepper jack cheese

4 slices colby jack cheese

1 tablespoon creole seasoning

1 teaspoon black pepper

1 teaspoon garlic powder

1 teaspoon onion powder

Extra virgin olive oil

Toothpicks

Directions:

1. Slice the peppers, and cut the cheese slices in half. Clean and dry the chicken. Preheat your grill to medium-high heat.

2. In a small bowl, mix together all the seasoning.

3. In the side of the chicken slice a slit that doesn't go all the way through.

4. Coat the chicken, and the slit with oil, and rub it in.

5. Season the entire chicken with the seasoning.

6. Place a piece of cheese in the slit, then a few peppers, and then another slice of cheese. Use the toothpicks to make sure the chicken is secure (about 3-4).

7. Grill the chicken for about 8 minutes a side.

8. Allow the chicken to sit for a few minutes, and then remove the toothpicks. Serve immediately.

Nutritional Info: Calories: 516 | Sodium: 1140 mg | Dietary Fiber: 5.2 g |
Total Fat: 22.6 g | Total Carbs: 16.0 g | Protein: 58.8 g.

Grilled Chicken Tacos

Servings: 12 Tacos | Prep Time: 6 Hours 20 Minutes | Cook Time: 17 Minutes

These tacos are flavorful and juicy thanks to the tomato lime marinade. Try topping them with your favorite ingredients

Ingredients:

3 medium tomatoes

1/3 cup fresh lime juice

1 cup water

1 teaspoon salt

2 pounds skinless boneless chicken thighs

2 tablespoons vegetable oil

1 teaspoon sweet paprika

1 teaspoon dried parsley

12 corn tortillas, warmed

Shredded Monterey Jack cheese for serving

Jarred salsa verde for serving

4 avocados for serving

1 onion for serving

3 tomatoes for serving

Cilantro for serving

Directions:

1. Coarsely chop the medium tomatoes.

2. Puree the chopped tomatoes, water, lime juice, and salt in a food processor blender. Put it in a big resealable freezer big with the chicken. Make sure the chicken is well coated, and place it in the refrigerator for at 6 hours.

3. Towards the end of the marinating process, preheat your grill to medium-high heat. Slice the avocado. Dice the tomatoes and onion. Chop the cilantro.

4. Take the chicken out of the bag and use paper towels to pat it dry. Use a brush to coat the chicken with the oil, and season with paprika, and parsley. Grill the chicken for about 15 minutes, flipping every few minutes. When cooked, let the chicken rest for 5 minutes. While the chicken is resting, warm the tortillas on the grill for 1 to 2 minutes.

5. Cut the chicken into pieces, and place an equal amount in each tortilla. Serve the tacos with the accompaniments.

Nutritional Info: Calories: 222 | Sodium: 272 mg | Dietary Fiber: 2.0 g |
Total Fat: 8.6 g | Total Carbs: 12.1 g | Protein: 23.6 g.

Mustard Soy Turkey Cutlets

Servings: 2 | Prep Time: 25 Minutes | Cook Time: 8 Minutes

The soy and mustard marinade gives the turkey a great sweet, and savory taste. Try this marinade with veal or chicken as well.

Ingredients:

2 – 4 turkey cutlets, depending on size, 12-ounce total

1 tablespoons soy sauce

1 tablespoons Dijon-style mustard

3 tablespoons white wine tarragon vinegar

3 tablespoons olive oil

1/2 teaspoon garlic powder

1/2 teaspoon rosemary

Directions:

1. Use a whisk to combine all the ingredients EXCEPT the turkey.

2. Put the marinade and the turkey in a bowl. Make sure to coat the turkey well with the marinade, and let it sit for at least 15 minutes.

3. While the turkey is marinating, preheat your grill to medium-high heat.

4. Grill the turkey for 3 to 4 minutes a side.

5. Serve immediately.

Nutritional Info: Calories: 250 | Sodium: 330 mg | Dietary Fiber: 0 g | Total Fat: 14.9 g | Total Carbs: 1.2 g | Protein: 25.4 g

Matt Jason

Grilled Chicken with Ancho Tequila Glaze

Servings: 6 | Prep Time: 17 Minutes | Cook Time: 25 Minutes

Ancho chilies are dried, ripe poblanos. They have a nice sweetness that pairs well with the flavor of the tequila.

Ingredients:

- 1 tablespoon ancho chili powder
- 1 1/2 teaspoons sugar
- 1 1/2 teaspoons granulated garlic
- 1 1/2 teaspoons ground cumin
- 1 1/2 teaspoons freshly ground black pepper
- 3/4 teaspoons kosher salt
- 12 bone-in chicken thighs (about 2 1/2 pounds)
- 1 1/2 tablespoons extra-virgin olive oil

- 6 tablespoons amber agave syrup
- 3 tablespoons tequila
- 1 1/2 tablespoons hot sauce
- 1 1/2 tablespoons butter
- 1 1/2 tablespoons fresh lime juice
- 1/4 teaspoon crushed red pepper
- Cooking spray
- 3 tablespoons fresh cilantro (optional)
- 6 lime wedges

Directions:

1. Remove the skin from the chicken. Chop the cilantro if using. Preheat your grill to medium-high, and grease it.

2. Combine the first 6 ingredients in a bowl. Toss the chicken with the spices, then add the oil, and toss again.

3. In a small saucepan, combine the agave, tequila, hot sauce, butter, lime juice, and crushed red pepper. Bring the mixture to a boil and then lower heat. Let the mixture cook for around 3 minutes. The mixture should reduce in size to 1/2 cup, and should be thicker.

4. Grill the chicken, meat side down for 10 minutes, brushing with the tequila glaze. Then flip it over, and cook for another 10 minutes, brushing again. Alternate sides if necessary for the next for 5 minutes, brushing throughout.

5. Serve with more glaze on the side. Garnish with cilantro if you'd like.

Nutritional Info: Calories: 512 | Sodium: 536 mg | Dietary Fiber: 0.9 g |
Total Fat: 20.8 g | Total Carbs: 21.0 g | Protein: 55.3 g.

Sriracha Maple Chicken Kebabs

Servings: 2 | Prep Time: 4 Hours | Cook Time: 16 Minutes

These kebabs have the perfect mix of spicy and sweet thanks to the sriracha and maple syrup. The soy sauce gives this dish the right amount of saltiness.

Ingredients:

 2 large chicken breasts, cubed
 1/4 cup soy sauce
 1/4 cup maple syrup
 1 tablespoon sriracha sauce

Directions:

1. Cube the chicken.

2. Use a whisk to mix together the remaining ingredients. Place the chicken and marinade in a large resealable plastic bag. Massage the marinade into the pieces of chicken. Let the chicken rest in the refrigerator for a minimum of 4 hours.

3. Towards the end of the marinating process, preheat your grill to high heat, and soak wood skewers in water for 20 minutes.

4. Place the chicken on the skewers, and grill for 7 to 8 minutes per side.

5. Serve immediately.

Nutritional Info: Calories: 238 | Sodium: 854 mg | Dietary Fiber: 0 g |
Total Fat: 4.7 g | Total Carbs: 28.9 g | Protein: 20.1 g.

Matt Jason

Grilled Half Duck with Raspberry Barbeque Sauce

Servings: 2-4 | Prep Time: 15 Minutes | Cook Time: 15-20 Minutes

The key to this dish is buying precooked roasted duck. It allows you to quickly grill the duck, and get the skin extra crispy.

Ingredients:

2 (12-14 ounce) packages roast half duck

Raspberry Barbecue Sauce:

1 1/2 cups fresh or frozen raspberries

3 tablespoons brown sugar

1 tablespoon balsamic vinegar

1 tablespoon molasses

1/2 teaspoon freshly squeezed lemon juice

1/4 teaspoon smoked paprika

1/8 teaspoon chipotle chili powder

1/8 teaspoon smoked sea salt (or regular)

1/8 teaspoon ground white pepper

1/8 teaspoon onion powder

1/8 teaspoon garlic powder

Directions:

1. Preheat your grill on medium heat.

2. While the grill is heating, place all the sauce ingredients into a nonstick sauce pan, and heat on medium heat. Bring the mixture to a boil, and then lower heat to let it simmer for 8 minutes. The sauce will thicken. Stir occasionally throughout.

3. Strain the mixture into a bowl.

Nutritional Info: Calories: 408 | Sodium: 175 mg | Dietary Fiber: 3.1 g |
Total Fat: 19.4 g | Total Carbs: 16.2 g | Protein: 40.6 g

Grilled Parmesan Ranch Chicken Foil Packets

Servings: 4 | Prep Time: 15 Minutes | Cook Time: 25 Minutes

This recipe lets you cook your entire meal at once, in an easy to clean up packet. The saw flavors everything with a wonderful tangy cheesy flavor.

Ingredients:

4 boneless skinless chicken breasts (4 to 5 ounce each)

1/2 teaspoon salt-free garlic-herb blend

1/2 cup reduced-fat ranch dressing

1/4 cup water

2 cups quartered small red potatoes

1 cup baby carrots, cut in half lengthwise

1/4 pound fresh green beans, trimmed

1/3 cup shredded parmesan cheese

Directions:

1. Preheat your grill to medium heat. Cut the potatoes into quarters. Cut the baby carrots in half lengthwise. Trim the green beans. Cut 4 pieces of aluminum foil that are 18x12. Oil them with cooking spray.

2. Season both sides of the chicken with herb blend. Put one piece of chicken in the middle of each piece of aluminum foil. Sprinkle 1 tablespoon of dressing on each piece of chicken.

3. Mix together the remaining dressing and water. Mix in the vegetables. Place an equal amount of vegetables on each piece of foil. Top everything with cheese.

4. Fold up 2 opposite sides of foil so they're touching. Fold the edges, and seal them. Fold again, and leave space for expansion. Do the same with the other sides.

5. Grill the packets for 10 minutes. Rotate the packets and continue to cook the packets for 5 to 15 minutes. The packets are done when the vegetables are tender, and the chicken is cooked through.

6. Carefully cut a hole in the packet to let steam escape, and then serve.

Nutritional Info: Calories: 300 | Sodium: 313 mg | Dietary Fiber: 2.4 g | Total Fat: 9.5 g | Total Carbs: 16.0 g | Protein: 36.5 g.

Hawaiian Chicken Skewers

Servings: 4-6 | Prep Time: 2-4 Hours | Cook Time: 10 Minutes

These skewers are packed with flavor thanks to the orange marmalade and soy sauce marinade. The pineapple, and vegetables compliment the flavor of the marinade well.

Ingredients:

1/2 cup chicken broth	12 skewers
3 tablespoons orange marmalade	1 purple onion
1 cup soy sauce	1 red bell pepper
1/2 teaspoon ground ginger	1/2 fresh pineapple
1/2 teaspoon garlic powder	Olive oil
3 skinless chicken breasts	1 tablespoon fresh cilantro

Directions:

1. Slice the onion, bell pepper, and pineapple into 1 inch chunks. Slice the chicken into 1 inch pieces. Chop the cilantro.

2. Mix the first 5 ingredients in a bowl. Put the chicken in a large resealable plastic bag, and pour the marinade in. Allow the chicken to marinate in the refrigerator for 2 to 4 hours.

3. If you're using wooden skewers soak them in water for 20 minutes.

4. Preheat your grill to medium-high heat. Place the chicken, pineapple, and vegetables on the skewers. Use a brush to lightly coat the grill with oil. Grill the skewers for 8 to 10, making sure to turn them every few minutes so the cook evenly.

5. Garnish with cilantro and serve.

Nutritional Info: Calories: 234 | Sodium: 1910 mg | Dietary Fiber: 5.2 g | Total Fat: 22.6 g | Total Carbs: 16.0 g | Protein: 58.8 g.

Honey Porter Chicken Skewers

Servings: 4 | Prep Time: 1 Hour 20 Minutes | Cook Time: 25 Minutes

The honey and porter work together to give a sweet and savory flavor. Porter is a rich dark beer that's full of flavor.

Ingredients:

2 cloves garlic

1/3 cup honey

1/2 cup porter or stout beer

1 teaspoon red pepper flakes

1/2 teaspoon Dijon mustard

1/4 cup soy sauce

1/4 teaspoon pepper

1 tablespoon olive oil

1/4 cup shallots (about 1 medium shallot)

6 boneless skinless chicken thigh fillets, cut into cubes

Oil for the grill

Cilantro for garnish (optional)

Directions:

1. Mince the garlic, and chop the shallots. Chop the cilantro if using. Cut the chicken into cubes.

2. Use a whisk to mix together the first 7 ingredients in a bowl. Add in the chicken and make sure it's well covered with the sauce. Refrigerate it, covered, for at least an hour. Towards the end of the marinating process soak wooden skewers in cold water for 20 minutes

3. Remove the chicken from the marinade, but keep the marinade. Place the chicken on the skewers and set aside.

4. Place the olive oil and shallots in a pot, and heat on medium heat. Cook the onions for around 5 minutes, until they become soft. Put in the marinade and let the mixture boil. Stir often, until the sauce becomes thick. This should take around 8 minutes.

5. Preheat your grill to medium-high heat, and brush it with a little oil.

6. Use a brush to coat the chicken with the new sauce, and put the skewers on the grill. Continue brushing the chicken with the sauce throughout the cooking process. Cook the skewers for about 10 minutes, making sure to turn them every few minutes.

7. Garnish with cilantro, and serve.

Nutritional Info: Calories: 330 | Sodium: 990 mg | Dietary Fiber: 0 g |
Total Fat: 11.7 g | Total Carbs: 27.0 g | Protein: 30.0 g

Matt Jason

Soy Grilled Quail Eggs with Sesame Salt

Servings: 24 Eggs | Prep Time: 40 Minutes | Cook Time: 5 Minutes

These eggs get a delicious nutty flavor from the sesame, and a sweetness from the soy. Grilling them gives them a nice smokiness.

Ingredients:

- 1 tablespoon sesame seeds (white and black)
- 1 teaspoon sea salt
- 24 quail eggs
- 2 tablespoons dark soy sauce
- 1 tablespoon olive oil

Directions:

1. Place the sesame seeds in a nonstick pan, and heat on medium heat. Toast them for 4 minutes, making sure to move them around so they toast evenly. Let them cool.

2. Place the cooled sesame seeds and salt in a blender or food processor. Pulse the mixture a few times to open up the sesame seeds.

3. Bring water to a boil in a medium pot. Put in the eggs, and lower the temperature to simmer for 2 minutes. Rinse the eggs off in cold water, and then peel them.

4. Combine the oil and soy in a big bowl, and toss the eggs in the mixture, carefully, until well coated. Let the eggs rest in the mixture for 30 minutes. While the eggs are marinating place a griddle pan on your grill, and heat the grill to medium-high heat.

5. Place the eggs on the griddle for 40 seconds, flipping them halfway through.

6. If desired place the eggs on skewers to serve. Serve with the sesame salt on the side.

Nutritional Info: Calories: 71 | Sodium: 215 mg | Dietary Fiber: 0 g | Total Fat: 5.2 g | Total Carbs: 0.5 g | Protein: 5.7 g

Spiced Grilled Lamb

Servings: 18 | Prep Time: 8 Hours 40 Minutes | Cook Time: 1 Hours 30 Minutes

The oregano gives the lamb a bold flavor that's tempered by the citrus flavors of the orange and lemon. Grilling the lamb brings out all of its natural flavors.

Ingredients:

1 (5-pound) boneless leg of lamb, trimmed

1/4 cup fresh lemon juice

3 tablespoons dried oregano

2 tablespoons plus 2 teaspoons ground cumin, divided

1 tablespoon coarse sea salt, divided

2 cups fresh orange juice

3 garlic cloves

1/4 cup olive oil

2 yellow onions, chopped

1 teaspoon crushed red pepper

Cooking spray

Directions:

1. Trim the fat from the lamb. Chop the onions.

2. Put the lamb in a large resealable plastic bag. Then put in the 2 tablespoons cumin, 2 teaspoons salt, lemon juice, and oregano. Make sure the lamb is well coated with the mixture. Refrigerate for at least 8 hours.

3. Use a blender or food processor to puree the orange juice, garlic, onions, and olive oil. Transfer to a bowl, and refrigerate for at least 8 hours.

4. Mix together the 2 teaspoons cumin, pepper, and 1 teaspoon salt.

5. Take the lamb out of the refrigerator, and let it sit for 30 minutes. Preheat your grill to medium heat. Use cooking spray to coat the grill.

6. Grill the lamb for 1 hour 30 minutes. Flip it over often, and use a brush to coat the lamb with the orange juice mixture. The internal temperature of the lamb will be 135F when ready.

7. Let the lamb sit for 15 minutes before cutting, and serving.

Nutritional Info: Calories: 283 | Sodium: 419 mg | Dietary Fiber: 0.8 g |
Total Fat: 12.4 g | Total Carbs: 5.2 g | Protein: 36.0 g

Matt Jason

Tandoori Grilled Chicken

Servings: 4 | Prep Time 1 Hour 15 Minutes | Cook Time: 15 Minutes

Tandoori is an Indian seasoning that gives the chicken a reddish color. It gives the chicken an aromatic full flavor.

Ingredients:

- 8-ounce plain nonfat yogurt
- 1 teaspoon lemon juice
- 2 tablespoons paprika
- 1 tablespoon garlic powder
- 1/4 teaspoon salt
- 1/2 teaspoon ground ginger
- 1/2 teaspoon cumin
- 1/2 teaspoon cayenne pepper
- 4 boneless skinless chicken breasts

Directions:

1. Combine all the ingredients EXCEPT for the chicken in a bowl.
2. Coat the chicken in the marinade, and let it rest for at least an hour, in the refrigerator, covered. Towards the end of the marinating process preheat the grill to medium-high heat.
3. Grill the chicken for 10 to 15 minutes, flipping halfway through. Make sure the chicken is completely cooked through.
4. Serve immediately.

Nutritional Info: Calories: 338 | Sodium: 315 mg | Dietary Fiber: 1.6 g | Total Fat: 12.1 g | Total Carbs: 7.9 g | Protein: 46.4 g.

CHAPTER

7

Seafood

Bacon Wrapped Scallops

Servings: 12 | Prep Time: 25 Minutes | Cook Time: 10 Minutes

This is a simple and delicious appetizer. The bacon gives a nice saltiness to the scallops.

Ingredients:

10 ounce scallops
12 pieces bacon
Cayenne pepper
Salt

Directions:

1. Preheat your grill to medium-high heat. If you're using wooden skewers soak them in cold water for 20 minutes.

2. Wrap the bacon around the scallops, and place them on the skewers. Add salt, and cayenne to the scallops to taste.

3. Grill for 10 minutes, making sure to turn throughout so that both the bacon, scallops are cooked.

4. Serve immediately.

Nutritional Info: Calories: 56 | Sodium: 184 mg | Dietary Fiber: 0 g | Total Fat: 2.9 g | Total Carbs: 0.9 g | Protein: 6.3 g

Blackened Cod with Grilled Pineapple

Servings: 4 | Prep Time: 15 Minutes | Cook Time: 10 Minutes

This dish has a great balance of heat and sweet. The blackened spices give this dish the heat, and the pineapple provides the sweet.

Ingredients:

4 (4-6 ounces) skinless center-cut cod fillets

1 fresh pineapple

1/4 cup butter (1/2 stick)

2 tablespoons garlic powder

1 1/2 tablespoons dried thyme leaves

1/4 teaspoon ground cayenne pepper

4 teaspoons smoked paprika

1 tablespoon ground coriander

1/2 teaspoon salt

Directions:

1. Preheat your grill to medium-high heat. Core the pineapple, and cut off the outside. Save half for another use, and slice the other half into 8 short wedges.

2. Microwave the butter until it melts, about 20 to 30 seconds. Mix together the thyme, garlic powder, paprika, coriander, cayenne, white pepper, and salt in a sauté pan. Heat the mixture for 3 to 4 minutes on medium heat, until it becomes fragrant. Let the mixture cool for a minute.

3. Coat the fish in the butter, and then coat it with the seasoning mixture.

4. Grill the fish for 2 to 3 minutes, covered. Grill for an additional 2 to 3 minutes. The fish is ready when you can flake it with a fork. Grill the pineapple at the same time as the fish. Grill for 3 to 4 minutes, flipping halfway through.

5. Top the fish with the pineapple, and serve.

Nutritional Info: Calories: 263 | Sodium: 464 mg | Dietary Fiber: 2.1 g |
Total Fat: 12.9 g | Total Carbs: 9.9 g | Protein: 27.3 g

Brown Sugar Soy Cod

Servings: 3 | Prep Time: 2 Hour 10 Minutes | Cook Time: 10 Minutes

This dish uses a simple marinade with things you probably have in your kitchen. The fish has a nice sweet, and citrusy flavor.

Ingredients:

> **2 tablespoons butter**
>
> **2 tablespoons brown sugar**
>
> **2 cloves garlic**
>
> **1 tablespoon lemon juice**
>
> **2 tablespoons soy sauce**
>
> **1/2 teaspoon pepper**
>
> **3 (6-ounce) cod fillets**

Directions:

1. Put all ingredients EXCEPT the cod in a small sauce pan, and heat on medium heat. Mix the ingredients together until the butter melts.

2. Let the mixture cool off, then add in the cod, and coat completely with the marinade. Place in the refrigerator covered for at least an hour and up to 2 hours.

3. Preheat the grill to medium-high heat, and lightly grease it. Use a brush to coat the cod with the sauce. Cook the cod for 10 minutes, flipping halfway through, basting with the sauce. The cod is cooked when you can flake it easily with a fork.

4. Serve immediately.

Nutritional Info: Calories: 280 | Sodium: 792 mg | Dietary Fiber: 0 g |
Total Fat: 9.2 g | Total Carbs: 7.7 g | Protein: 39.8 g

Grilled Blackened Tilapia

Servings: 4 | Prep Time: 10 Minutes | Cook Time: 4 Minutes

This dish has some heat to it thanks to the cayenne. Grilling the tilapia makes is nice and crusty.

Ingredients:

1 pound tilapia	1 tablespoon butter

Blackening Rub:

3 tablespoons paprika	1 teaspoon dry oregano
1 teaspoon salt	1/2 teaspoon garlic powder
1 tablespoon onion powder	1/4 -1 teaspoon cayenne pepper to taste
1 teaspoon black pepper	
1 teaspoon dry thyme	

Directions:

1. Preheat your grill to high.

2. Mix together all the rub ingredients.

3. Wash and dry the tilapia.

4. Put the butter in the microwave for 15 seconds to melt it. Use a brush to coat the tilapia with the butter.

5. Coat the tilapia well with the rub.

6. Place the tilapia in a grill basket or put a griddle pan on the grill. If using the griddle place 1 tablespoon of vegetable oil on it.

7. Grill the tilapia for 4 minutes, flipping exactly halfway through.

8. Serve when done.

Nutritional Info: Calories: 146 | Sodium: 645 mg | Dietary Fiber: 2.6 g |
Total Fat: 4.7 g | Total Carbs: 5.5 g | Protein: 22.3 g

Matt Jason

Grilled Fish Tacos

Servings: 6 | Prep Time: 50 Minutes | Cook Time: 6 Minutes

These fish tacos don't taste fishy at thanks to the marinade and the slaw. The slaw and the avocado give these tacos a wonderful texture.

Ingredients:

Tacos:

1 pound tilapia, cod or mahi mahi fillets

2 tablespoons canola oil

1 1/2 tablespoons fresh lime juice

1 clove garlic

1 1/2 teaspoons chili powder

1/2 teaspoon ground cumin

1/2 teaspoon ground paprika

1/8 teaspoon cayenne pepper (optional)

Salt and pepper

6 corn or flour tortillas

1 large avocado, sliced

Sour cream, cotija cheese, hot sauce or salsa, for serving (optional)

Slaw:

1/2 small red cabbage (8 ounce)

1/4 cup cilantro

3/4 cups red onion

1 1/2 tablespoons lime juice

1 tablespoon canola oil

Directions:

1. Mince the garlic. Slice the avocado. Core and thinly slice the cabbage. Chop the cilantro. Thinly slice the onion.

2. Combine the lime juice, garlic, chili pepper, salt and pepper, cumin, cayenne, and paprika. Put the fish in a large resealable plastic bag, and add in the combined marinade. Make sure the fish is well coated with the marinade, and place in the refrigerator for 20 to 30 minutes. Towards the end of the marinating process preheat your grill to medium-high heat, and lightly grease the grill.

3. While the fish is marinating. Put the onion, cilantro, and cabbage in a bowl. Add in the canola oil, lime juice, and salt and pepper to taste. Mix all the ingredients together.

4. Grill the fish for about 6 minutes, flipping halfway through. Slice the fish into strips, and place them in tortillas with avocado, and slaw. Serve immediately.

Nutritional Info: Calories: 278 | Sodium: 115 mg | Dietary Fiber: 5.6 g | Total Fat: 14.9 g | Total Carbs: 21.9 g | Protein: 17.7 g

Grilled Fish Tostadas

Serving: 4 | Prep Time: 10 Minutes | Cook Time: 8 Minutes

These tostadas are a healthy easy meal to make. Use your favorite salsa to give it a special touch.

Ingredients:

4 white fish fillets (halibut, tilapia, etc.)

1/2 jar of medium salsa

8 corn tortillas

Mashed avocado or guacamole

Cheese, jalapenos, lettuce (optional)

Salt, pepper to taste

Directions:

1. Preheat your grill to medium heat. Preheat your oven to 400F.

2. Put the fish in the middle of a big piece of aluminum foil. Use the salsa to complete coat, and cover the fish. Fold the sides of the aluminum foil over the fish, and seal it closed.

3. Grill the packets for 6 to 8 minutes. Make sure the fish is completely cooked before taking it off the grill.

4. While the packets are grilling, put the tortillas on a baking sheet, and put them in the oven. Bake them until they're crispy, but not yet brown, 6 to 8 minutes. Allow the tortillas to cool off for about 1 minute.

5. Spread the avocado/guacamole on the crispy tortillas.

6. Slice up the fish, and place it on the tortillas. Put the salsa from the aluminum foil on top of the fish, and serve.

Nutritional Info: Calories: 157 | Sodium: 295 mg | Dietary Fiber: 4.1 g |
Total Fat: 3.5 g | Total Carbs: 24.7 g | Protein: 8.8 g

Grilled Halibut with Lemon Basil Dressing

Servings: 4 | Prep Time: 5 Minutes | Cook Time: 8 Minutes

The dressing compliments this piece of fish wonderfully. The dressing has a delicate, citrus flavor. Double the amount if you like lots of sauce.

Ingredients:

2 1/2 tablespoons fresh lemon juice

2 tablespoons extra-virgin olive oil

2 garlic cloves

1/2 teaspoon lemon peel

3 tablespoons fresh basil or 3 teaspoons dried

2 teaspoons capers

4 (5-6 ounce) halibut steaks (about 3/4-inch-thick)

Directions:

1. Grate the lemon peel. Crush the garlic. Drain the capers. Thinly slice the basil. Preheat your grill to medium-high heat.

2. Use a whisk to mix together lemon juice, olive oil, garlic, and lemon peel. Mix in the basil, and capers. Salt and pepper to taste.

3. Salt and pepper the fish to taste. Use a brush to coat the fish with half of the dressing. Grill the fish for about 8 minutes, flipping halfway through.

4. Put the fish on plates. Whisk the dressing again if necessary. Top the fish with the dressing, and serve.

Nutritional Info: Calories: 3759 | Sodium: 1872 mg | Dietary Fiber: 0 g | Total Fat: 79.2 g | Total Carbs: 0.5 g | Protein: 714.8 g

Grilled Lime Shrimp in Corn

Servings: 4 | Prep Time: 15 Minutes | Cook Time: 10 Minutes

Making packets out of aluminum foil is great way to seal in all the flavors. This also a great dish to make when you're camping. You can cook the packets right on the camp fire.

Ingredients:

 1/3 cup fresh lime juice

 1/4 cup fresh orange juice

 2 tablespoons low-sodium soy sauce

 2 tablespoons honey

 2 garlic cloves

 2 teaspoons grated fresh ginger

 2 tablespoons sugar

 1 teaspoon ground coriander seeds

 1/4 teaspoon black pepper

 2 ears corn

 1 1/2 pounds large shrimp

 4 cups cooked couscous

Directions:

1. Mince the garlic. Cut the corn into 4 pieces crosswise. Peel and devein the shrimp. Preheat your grill to medium-high heat.

2. Mix the first 9 ingredients in a bowl.

3. Use 2, 24-inch-long pieces of aluminum foil to create a package for the shrimp and corn.

4. Mix the shrimp and corn with the spice mixture. Cover the shrimp and corn, and pinch the ends closed. Cover the package with a 3rd piece of aluminum foil.

5. Place the packets on the grill, and cook for 10 minutes.

6. Put the couscous on plates, and place the shrimp and corn on top of it.

Nutritional Info: Calories: 888 | Sodium: 672 mg | Dietary Fiber: 9.8 g |
Total Fat: 1.4 g | Total Carbs: 162.6 g | Protein: 55.8 g

Grilled Lobster Tails with Garlic Thyme Butter

Servings: 4 | Prep Time: 15 Minutes | Cook Time: 10 Minutes

This is a simple, and quick dish to make. The garlic thyme butter compliments the rich taste of the lobster well.

Ingredients:

4 (4 - 5 ounce) lobster tails

2 tablespoons (28g) butter, melted

2 cloves garlic, minced

1 teaspoon fresh thyme, coarsely chopped

1/8 teaspoon ground pepper

1/2 teaspoon salt

Directions:

1. Chop the thyme, and mince the garlic. Place the garlic in the microwave for about 20 seconds on high to melt it.

2. Slice the lobster tail along the right of the tail, and then the left. Then slice the back, and remove the shell. Rinse, clean, dry the tails.

3. Loosen the meat from shell, but make sure the tail is still attached.

4. Use aluminum foil to cover the tail.

5. Mix together all the ingredients together EXCEPT for the lobster. Use a brush to coat the lobster meat with the butter.

6. Grill the lobster for 5 minutes, and then brush it with more butter. Grill for an additional 5 minutes.

7. Remove the aluminum foil, and serve.

Nutritional Info: Calories: 180 | Sodium: 1020 mg | Dietary Fiber: 0 g | Total Fat: 6.9 g | Total Carbs: 0.7 g | Protein: 27.1 g

Grilled Calamari

Serving: 4 | Prep Time: 20 Minutes | Cook Time: 10 Minutes

This dish gives you a chance to try calamari that's not deep fried. It's simply grilled with a little citrus for a subtle flavor.

Ingredients:

1 pound calamari, tubes only

Salt and pepper

Extra virgin olive oil

1 lime, cut into wedges

Few sprigs fresh parsley, finely minced

Bamboo skewers, soaked

Directions:

1. Soak the skewers for 20 minutes in cold water. Preheat your grill to medium-high heat. Finely mince the parsley. Cut the lime into wedges. Rinse and use a paper towel to pat the calamari dry.

2. Salt and pepper both sides of the calamari to taste. Place them on the skewers.

3. Grill the skewers for 4 minutes a side.

4. Top the skewers with olive oil, lime juice and parsley. Serve immediately.

Nutritional Info: Calories: 113 | Sodium: 90 mg | Dietary Fiber: 0.8 g | Total Fat: 1.6 g | Total Carbs: 6.1 g | Protein: 17.9 g

Matt Jason

Grilled Mahi with Avocado and Corn Salsa

Servings: 4 | Prep Time: 15 Minutes | Cook Time: 10 Minutes

This is a delightful and easy dish to make. The avocado gives the dish a nice creaminess, and the poblano gives it a little heat.

Ingredients:

4 mahi mahi fillets
2 tablespoons olive oil
2 teaspoons ground cumin
2 teaspoons chili powder
1/2 teaspoon salt
1/4 teaspoon pepper

For Salsa:

2 fresh ears of corn
1 poblano pepper
1 firm ripe avocado
1/3 cup purple onion
1 tablespoon sugar
1 tablespoon vinegar
1/2 teaspoon salt
1/4 teaspoon pepper

Directions:

1. Shuck the corn, and take the corn off the cob. Chop and seed the poblano. Cube the avocado. Chop the onion. Preheat your grill to medium heat.

2. Combine all the salsa ingredients in a bowl, and refrigerate until ready to serve.

3. Mix the salt pepper, olive oil, cumin, and chili powder in a small bowl.

4. Use a brush to coat the mahi with it.

5. Place the mahi in your grill, and cook it for about 4 minutes a side.

6. Plate and serve topped with salsa or on the side.

Nutritional Info: Calories: 218 | Sodium: 633 mg | Dietary Fiber: 4.5 g |
Total Fat: 17.5 g | Total Carbs: 11.6 g | Protein: 6.5 g

Grilled Oysters

Servings: 2 | Prep Time: 10 Minutes | Cook Time: 10 Minutes

This flavorful dish is a New Orleans favorite. The oysters are topped with a delicious garlic butter, and cheese.

Ingredients:

12 oysters on the half shell

3 tablespoons parsley, chopped

2 tablespoons lemon juice (~1/2 lemon)

1/4 cup parmesan, grated

1 teaspoon worcestershire sauce

1 stick butter

2 cloves garlic

Salt, pepper and cayenne to taste

Directions:

1. Bring the butter up to room temperature. Grate the garlic. Chop the parsley. Preheat your grill to medium heat.

2. Combine the lemon juice, 1 tablespoon parsley, butter, 1/4 cup cheese, Worcestershire, cayenne, salt, and pepper.

3. Put the oysters on the grill, shell side down. Cook the oysters until they start to bubble, and then 1 tablespoon of the cheese mixture to each, and add more cheese. Cook until the cheese melts, and turns golden.

4. Top with the 2 tablespoons parsley, and serve with remaining butter on the side.

Nutritional Info: Calories: 278 | Sodium: 353 mg | Dietary Fiber: 0 g | Total Fat: 26.9 g | Total Carbs: 2.7 g | Protein: 7.6 g

Matt Jason

Grilled Salmon Salad with Avocado Greek Yogurt Ranch Dressing

Servings: 4 | Prep Time: 20 Minutes | Cook Time: 6 Minutes

This tasty dish is very healthy. The dressing taste like just like regular ranch, but it's so much healthier because of the avocado and Greek yogurt.

Ingredients:

4 (5 – 6 ounce) salmon fillets, skinless

1 teaspoon ancho chili powder

1 teaspoon ground cumin

1/2 teaspoon paprika

1/2 teaspoon onion powder

1 1/2 tablespoons olive oil, plus more for grill

Salt and freshly ground black pepper

1 lime

Salad:

1 head romaine lettuce

10 ounces grape tomatoes

1 cucumber

1 1/2 cups fresh corn

1/2 red onion

1/4 cup cilantro leaves (optional)

4 ounce queso fresco or feta cheese

Avocado Greek yogurt ranch dressing

1 cup plain fat free or low-fat Greek yogurt

1 medium avocado

1 1/2 tablespoons fresh lime juice

1 clove garlic

2 tablespoons fresh parsley (or 2 teaspoon dried)

1 /2 teaspoon fresh dill, to taste (or 1/2 teaspoon dried)

2 teaspoon fresh chives (or 3/4 teaspoon dried)

1/2 teaspoon onion powder

Salt and freshly ground black pepper, to taste

Up to 6 tablespoons milk, as needed (for a slightly richer dressing sub 2 Tablespoon olive oil for some of the milk)

Directions:

Dressing:

1. Peel and core the avocado. Chop the parsley, dill, and chives.

2. Place all the ingredients EXCEPT the milk in a food processor, or blender. Pulse until the ingredients are well combined. Put in 1 tablespoon of milk at a time until your desired consistency is reached. Place in the refrigerator.

Salmon and Salad:

3. Preheat your grill to medium-high heat. Slice the onion, and rinse it with cold water. Halve the lime, and grape tomatoes. Peel and chop the cucumber.

4. Mix together the onion powder, paprika, chili powder, and cumin using a whisk. Use a brush to coat the salmon with olive oil, then salt and pepper to taste. Season the

salmon with the spice mixture. Grease the grill with olive oil. Grill the salmon for 6 minutes, and flip halfway through.

5.   Top the salmon with fresh lime juice.

6.   Combine the salad ingredients on 4 plates. Top with the salmon, and then drizzle with dressing. Serve immediately.

Nutritional Info: Calories: 605 | Sodium: 282 mg | Dietary Fiber: 7.3 g |
Total Fat: 36.4 g | Total Carbs: 31.5 g | Protein: 46.4 g

Matt Jason

Grilled Salmon with Maple Sriracha Lime Glaze

Servings: 2 | Prep Time: 15 Minutes | Cook Time: 8-10 Minutes

The glaze gives this beautiful fish a full flavor. The maple syrup helps balance the spiciness of the sriracha, and the lime gives it a little acidity.

Ingredients:

2 (6-ounce) skinless salmon about (6-ounce each)
3 - 4 teaspoons olive oil
2 teaspoons fish rub seasoning
Cooking spray

Glaze:

3 tablespoons maple syrup
1 1/2 tablespoons fresh squeezed lime juice
2 - 3 teaspoons Sriracha Rooster Sauce

Directions:

1. Pat the salmon dry. Coat both sides of the salmon with oil, and then the fish rub. Allow the salmon to come up to room temperature.

2. Spray your grill with cooking spray, and preheat your grill to high.

3. Use a whisk to mix the glaze ingredients. Use a brush to coat both sides of the room temperature salmon with the glaze.

4. Place the salmon on the grill, and turn the heat down to medium-high heat. Grill the salmon for 4 minutes, and then rotate it to get cross grill marks. Grill for another 4 minutes, and then flip the salmon over, and grill it for another 1 to 2 minutes. The salmon will be firm when touched when it's ready.

5. Serve immediately with a side of the sauce.

Nutritional Info: Calories: 390 | Sodium: 130 mg | Dietary Fiber: 0 g | Total Fat: 19.9 g | Total Carbs: 22.3 g | Protein: 33.0 g

Grilled Sardines with Chopped Herbs

Servings: 4 | Prep Time: 35 Minutes | Cook Time: 4 Minutes

The herbs give this dish a ton of flavor. The lemon gives it a little acidity the balance the flavor of the herbs and the fish.

Ingredients:

8 sardines

1/2 tablespoon rosemary

1 tablespoon parsley

1 garlic clove

1/2 tablespoon pitted green olives

1/2 tablespoon capers

1/2 teaspoon sea salt

1/4 teaspoon freshly ground black pepper

1 teaspoon lemon zest

Extra virgin olive oil, for brushing and serving

Lemon wedges, to serve

Directions:

1. Soak the wood skewers in cold water for 20 minutes. Chop the rosemary, parsley, and capers. Finely chop the garlic, and olives. Finely grate the lemon zest. Clean and trim the sardines. Preheat your grill to high.

2. Combine the first 8 ingredients in a bowl. Put the sardines on the skewers. Place them on a rimmed baking sheet and drizzle them with olive oil. Salt and pepper to taste.

3. Grill the sardine for 2 minutes a side.

4. Slather the sardines with the herb mixture, and top with a little olive oil. Serve with the lemon wedges.

Nutritional Info: Calories: 107 | Sodium: 543 mg | Dietary Fiber: 0 g | Total Fat: 9.2 g | Total Carbs: 1.0 g | Protein: 12.0 g

Grilled Salmon and Lemon Kebobs

Servings: 4 | Prep Time: 20 Minutes | Cook Time: 10 Minutes

These healthy kebobs are filled with light fresh flavor. The citrus flavor from the lemon pairs well with the salmon.

Ingredients:

2 tablespoons fresh oregano

2 teaspoon sesame seeds

1 teaspoon ground cumin

1/4 teaspoon crushed red pepper flakes

1 1/2 pounds skinless wild salmon fillet

2 lemons

Olive oil cooking spray

1 teaspoon kosher salt

16 bamboo skewers

Directions:

1. Chop the oregano. Cut the salmon into 1 inch pieces. Slice the lemons into very thin rounds. Soak the skewers in cold water for 20 minutes. Preheat your grill to medium heat, and grease it.

2. Combine the first 4 ingredients, and set aside.

3. Place the salmon and lemon slices on pairs of skewers, Start and end with the salmon. Fold lemons in half when putting them on the skewers. Use the olive oil spray to coat the salmon, and then season with the herb mixture, and salt.

4. Grill the skewers for about 8 to 10 minutes. Make sure to rotate the skewers throughout. The skewers are ready when the fish turns opaque.

Nutritional Info: Calories: 254 | Sodium: 659 mg | Dietary Fiber: 2.4 g | Total Fat: 11.7 g | Total Carbs: 5.8 g | Protein: 34.1 g

Grilled Seabass with Garlic and Parsley Butter

Servings: 6 | Prep Time: 20 Minutes | Cook Time: 20 Minutes

The lemon pepper gives this dish hint of citrus that highlights the flavor of the seabass. The butter helps keep the fish moist and infuses it with a delicious garlic flavor.

Ingredients:

- 1/4 teaspoon garlic powder
- 1/4 teaspoon onion powder
- 1/4 teaspoon paprika
- Lemon pepper to taste
- Sea salt to taste
- 2 pounds halibut
- 3 tablespoons butter
- 2 garlic cloves
- 2 tablespoons flat leaf Italian parsley
- 1 1/2 tablespoons extra virgin olive oil

Directions

1. Chop the parsley, and garlic. Preheat your grill to high heat.

2. Mix together the lemon pepper, salt, garlic powder, onion powder, and paprika. Season both sides of the fish with it.

3. Melt the butter with the garlic and parsley, in a small sauce pan, on medium heat. Take the pan off the heat when the butter melts.

4. Lightly grease your grill. Grill the fish for 7 minutes, and then flip it over. Carefully pour the melted butter on the fish. Cook for another 7 minutes.

5. Top with a little olive oil, and serve.

Nutritional Info: Calories: 3047 | Sodium: 1515 mg | Dietary Fiber: 0 g | Total Fat: 68.0 g | Total Carbs: 0.3 g | Protein: 571.8 g

Grilled Halibut with Garlic and Parsley Butter

Servings: 6 | Prep Time: 20 Minutes | Cook Time: 20 Minutes

The lemon pepper gives this dish hint of citrus that highlights the flavor of the seabass. The butter helps keep the fish moist and infuses it with a delicious garlic flavor.

Ingredients:

1/4 teaspoon garlic powder

1/4 teaspoon onion powder

1/4 teaspoon paprika

Lemon pepper to taste

Sea salt to taste

2 pounds halibut

3 tablespoons butter

2 garlic cloves

2 tablespoons flat leaf Italian parsley

1 1/2 tablespoons extra virgin olive oil

Directions:

1. Chop the parsley, and garlic. Preheat your grill to high heat.

2. Mix together the lemon pepper, salt, garlic powder, onion powder, and paprika. Season both sides of the fish with it.

3. Melt the butter with the garlic and parsley, in a small sauce pan, on medium heat. Take the pan off the heat when the butter melts.

4. Lightly grease your grill. Grill the fish for 7 minutes, and then flip it over. Carefully pour the melted butter on the fish. Cook for another 7 minutes. Top with a little olive oil, and serve.

Nutritional Info: Calories: 6094 | Sodium: 2990 mg | Dietary Fiber: 0 g | Total Fat: 135.9 g | Total Carbs: 0.6 g | Protein: 1143.6 g

Grilled Pesto Mozzarella Pizza with Arugula

Servings: 8 | Prep Time: 5 Minutes | Cook Time: 11 Minutes

This pizza is very quick to make because you start with a precooked crust. The arugula salad on top gives the pizza a nice lemon pepper flavor.

Ingredients:

1 pre-cooked 12-inch whole wheat pizza crust

1/2 cup basil pesto

8-ounce part-skim fresh mozzarella

12-ounce baby arugula

Zest and juice of one lemon

1 tablespoon olive oil

Salt and pepper to taste

Grated parmesan cheese and red chili flakes for garnish

Directions:

1. Cut the mozzarella into 1/2-inch slices. Preheat your grill to medium heat.

2. Cover the crust with the pesto and top it with the mozzarella.

3. Grill the pizza for 8 to 11 minutes. The pizza is ready when the crust is warmed through, and the cheese is melted.

4. Mix the arugula, lemon juice, zest, and olive oil during the grilling process. Then salt and pepper to taste.

5. Top the pizza with the arugula. Top with parmesan, and season with red pepper flakes if desired.

Nutritional Info: Calories: 124 | Sodium: 228 mg | Dietary Fiber: 1.0 g |
Total Fat: 7.3 g | Total Carbs: 6.1 g | Protein: 9.7 g

Matt Jason

Grilled Shrimp Tacos with Avocado Slaw and Mango Salsa

Servings: 4 | Prep Time: 23 Minutes | Cook Time: 2 Minutes

These are the perfect tacos for summer. The mango salsa gives them a summery tropical flavor that pair well with the shrimp.

Ingredients:

Avocado Slaw:

8 ounces coleslaw mix	Juice of a lime
1/2 of a 7-ounce container guacamole	1 tablespoon chopped cilantro
3 tablespoons plain non-fat Greek yogurt	Kosher salt and black pepper to taste

Mango Salsa:

2 mangos, peeled and diced	Juice of a lime
1/3 cup diced red onion	1 teaspoon honey (optional)
1/4 cup packed cilantro leaves, chopped	1/4 teaspoon chili powder
	Kosher salt and black pepper to taste

Shrimp:

1 pound large raw peeled and deveined shrimp	1/4 teaspoon cumin
1/4 teaspoon chili powder	Kosher salt and black pepper to taste
1/4 teaspoon smoked paprika	Corn tortillas for serving the tacos

Directions:

1. Chop the cilantro. Peel and devein the shrimp. Peel and dice the mango. Dice the onion. Preheat your grill to medium-high heat and grease it. If using wood skewers soak them in cold water for 20 minutes.

2. Mix all of the slaw ingredients together EXCEPT for the slaw mix in a big bowl. Then mix in the slaw mix until it's well-coated. Then place the mixture in the refrigerator covered.

3. Mix all the mango salsa ingredients together until they're well combined and place in the refrigerator, covered.

4. Toss the shrimp together with the spices until they're completely coated. Place them on the skewers.

5. Grill the shrimp for 2 minutes, flipping halfway through. The shrimp will turn pink when they're ready.

6. Grill the tortillas to crisp them, and give them a little char.

7.   Divide the shrimp evenly among the tortillas.

8.   Top the shrimp with slaw, and mango salsa. Serve immediately.

Nutritional Info: Calories: 259 | Sodium: 423 mg | Dietary Fiber: 1.9 g |
Total Fat: 10.9 g | Total Carbs: 22.2 g | Protein: 23.7 g

Matt Jason

Grilled Shrimp with Roasted Garlic Cilantro Sauce

Servings: 4 | Prep Time: 15 Minutes | Cook Time: 16 Minutes

This dish has a delicious Mediterranean flavor. It gets a little kick of spice from the chili sauce/flakes.

Ingredients:

> 1 1/2 pounds uncooked shrimp
> Salt and pepper
> Olive oil

Roasted Garlic-Cilantro Sauce:

> 1 small head garlic
> 1 cup fresh cilantro leaves
> 1 lime
> 1 tablespoon dry white wine
> 3 tablespoons olive oil
> 2 tablespoons chili sauce (or 1 tablespoon dry chili flakes)

Directions:

1. Cut the top off the head of garlic. Juice the lime. Chop the cilantro. Preheat your oven to 400F. Peel and devein the shrimp.

2. Use a paper towel to dry the shrimp. Salt and pepper to taste. Refrigerate the shrimp until it's time to grill.

3. Coat the garlic well with olive oil. Place the garlic in the oven for 10 to 15 minutes. The garlic will smell fragrant, and be slightly tender. Peel the garlic, and mince it finely.

4. Use a whisk to combine all of the sauce ingredients and set aside.

5. Preheat the grill to medium-high heat, and lightly grease it. Brush the shrimp with olive oil, and grill it for 6 to 8 minutes, flipping halfway through.

6. Serve the shrimp with the sauce on the side.

Nutritional Info: Calories: 303 | Sodium: 647 mg | Dietary Fiber: 0.6 g |
Total Fat: 13.5 g | Total Carbs: 5.0 g | Protein: 39.0 g

Grilled Swordfish with Lemon Basil Butter

Servings: 4 | Prep Time: 15 minutes | Cook Time: 9 Minutes

Swordfish is a firm fish, so it grills well. The lemon basil butter gives the fish a nice mix of aromatic, sweet, and acidity.

Ingredients:

2 swordfish steaks, 1-inch thick (about 2-pound)
Juice of 1/2 lemon
Extra virgin olive oil
Kosher salt and freshly ground black pepper

For the Lemon Basil Butter:

4 tablespoons unsalted butter
1 teaspoon freshly squeezed lemon juice
Zest of 1 lemon
1/2 clove garlic
1/4 teaspoon salt
2 tablespoons fresh basil

Directions:

1. Preheat your grill to high heat. Leave the butter out to soften. Mince the garlic, and basil. Slice the swordfish in half.

2. Coat the fish with the juice of 1/2 lemon and let it rest for 1 minute. Rub the fish with olive oil, and salt and pepper to taste.

3. Mix all the lemon basil butter ingredients together in a bowl.

4. Grease the grill.

5. Grill the fish for 7 to 9 minutes, flipping halfway through. The fish will be opaque when done.

6. Place 1 tablespoon butter on top of the fish when it's right off the grill. Let the fish sit for 2 to 3 minutes, and then serve.

Nutritional Info: Calories: 3759 | Sodium: 1872 mg | Dietary Fiber: 0 g | Total Fat: 79.2 g | Total Carbs: 0.5 g | Protein: 714.8 g

Lemongrass Shrimp Skewers

Servings: 4 | Prep Time: 2 Hours 20 Minutes | Cook Time: 5 Minutes

This dish is beautifully fragrant thanks to the lemongrass, and ginger. The brown sugar gives a nice touch of sweetness to balance the spiciness of the ginger.

Ingredients:

- 1/2 cup coconut milk
- 1/4 cup fish sauce
- 3 tablespoons firmly packed light brown sugar
- 1 teaspoon grated fresh ginger
- 2 tablespoons fresh cilantro
- 1 tablespoon curry powder
- 1 1/2-pounds medium shrimp
- 4 lemongrass stalks
- Store-bought peanut sauce for dipping

Directions:

1. Peel and devein the shrimp. Chop the cilantro.

2. Mix the first 6 ingredients together in a big bowl. Put in the shrimp, and toss them in the mixture until well coated. Cover the bowl, and refrigerate it for 2 hours.

3. Cut the top and root bottom off the lemongrass. Slice the lemongrass in half lengthwise. Place the marinated shrimp, and lemongrass on skewers.

4. Preheat your grill to high heat. Grease it with cooking spray. Grill the shrimp for 2 minutes a side. The shrimp will be opaque when it's done.

5. Place the shrimp on a warmed plate. Serve with the peanut sauce on the side.

Nutritional Info: Calories: 275 | Sodium: 782 mg | Dietary Fiber: 1.2 g | Total Fat: 9.4 g | Total Carbs: 11.5 g | Protein: 38.4 g

Grilled Walleye Fillets

Servings: 2-3 | Prep Time: 10 Minutes | Cook Time: 14 Minutes

This is a quick and easy dish to make. Choose your favorite herb blend, and put everything in a foil packet to grill. The best part is there's no mess to cleanup.

Ingredients:

1 pound walleye fillets

2 (12x12) sheets of aluminum foil

5 tablespoons butter

1 pinch seasoning salt

1 pinch herb seasoning blend of your choice

Directions:

1. Preheat your grill to medium-high heat. Place the butter in the microwave for 20 seconds on high or until it melts.

2. Put the walleye in the center of one of the pieces of aluminum foil, skin side down. Use a brush to coat the fish with butter. Season the fish with herb blend, and seasoning salt to taste. Cover with the other piece of aluminum foil, and seal the edges to create a packet.

3. Grill the packets for 14 minutes, flipping halfway through. The fish is done when you can flake it easily with a fork.

4. Serve with side dish of your choice.

Nutritional Info: Calories: 520 | Sodium: 991 mg | Dietary Fiber: 0.8 g | Total Fat: 37.8 g | Total Carbs: 25.7 g | Protein: 22.4 g

Matt Jason

Jerk Shrimp and Pineapple Skewers

Servings: 4 | Prep Time: 50 Minutes | Cook Time: 10 Minutes

Jerk is a spicy Caribbean marinate. It has a ton of flavor, and pairs well with the sweetness of the pineapple.

Ingredients:

1 pound (20-25 or 16-20) shrimp

1/2 cup jerk marinade

2 slices pineapple

Jerk Marinade:

1 scotch bonnet pepper (add more if desired)

2 cloves garlic

1 tablespoon grated ginger

2 green onions

1 tablespoon thyme

1 tablespoon allspice

3/4 teaspoons nutmeg

3/4 teaspoons cinnamon

1 teaspoon pepper

1 tablespoon brown sugar

1 tablespoon oil

2 tablespoons white vinegar

2 tablespoons soy sauce

1 tablespoon dark rum

1/2 orange

1 lime

Directions:

1. Peel and devein the shrimp. Slice the pineapple into 1/2 inch chunks. Chop the thyme. Juice and zest the orange, and lime.

2. Puree all the jerk ingredients in a blender or food processor. Divide the marinade into 2 equal parts.

3. Place the shrimp in half the marinade, make sure it well coated, and let it rest for at least 20 minutes. If you're using wood skewers, soak them in cold water for 20 minutes. Preheat your grill to medium-high heat.

4. Place the shrimp, and pineapple on the skewers. Grill them for 4 to 6 minutes, and flip them halfway through.

5. Serve with more jerk marinade, or save it for later.

Nutritional Info: Calories: 223 | Sodium: 734 mg | Dietary Fiber: 2.2 g |
Total Fat: 5.9 g | Total Carbs: 13.0 g | Protein: 27.4 g

Lime White Pepper Grilled Scallop Skewers

Servings 4 | Prep Time: 25 Minutes | Cook Time: 20 Minutes

The lime and white pepper give this dish a nice spice, and citrus flavor. The bell pepper adds a nice smokiness.

Ingredients:

> 2 roasted red bell peppers
>
> 2 tablespoons extra-virgin olive oil
>
> 2 garlic cloves
>
> 1 lime
>
> Salt and freshly ground white peppercorns, to taste
>
> 16 large sea scallops

Directions:

1. Peel, deseed, and halve the peppers. Finely mince the garlic. Juice and zest the lime. Rinse and pat the scallops dry.

2. Puree the bell peppers in a food processor or blender.

3. Heat the olive oil, on medium-low heat, in a saucepan. Put in the garlic, and cook it for about 1 minute. It will turn golden brown. Put in the lime juice, salt, white pepper, and pepper puree. And use a whisk to mix all the ingredients. Keep the mixture warm.

4. Preheat your grill to high heat.

5. Mix salt, white pepper, and lime zest. Put the shrimp on metal skewers, and place them on the grill. Grill the shrimp for 4 to 8 minutes, flipping them halfway through. The shrimp will be opaque when cooked. Put the cooked skewers on a warm plate.

6. Salt and pepper the bell pepper sauce to taste, if necessary. Coat the shrimp with desired amount of sauce, and serve.

Nutritional Info: Calories: 191 | Sodium: 235 mg | Dietary Fiber: 1.8 g |
Total Fat: 8.1 g | Total Carbs: 8.7 g | Protein: 20.9 g

Skillet Grilled Chorizo and Seafood Paella

Servings: 6 | Prep Time: 10 Minutes | Cook Time: 45 Minutes

This dish is so easy because you cook everything in one pot. Grilling the paella gives everything a wonderful smokiness.

Ingredients:

4 ounces Spanish chorizo

2 small skinless chicken thighs or breast

2 cups jasmine or basmati rice

2 tablespoons olive oil

1/2 small sweet onion

2 cloves garlic

3 - 4 heirloom tomatoes or 1 (15-ounce) can whole peeled tomatoes

1 (8-ounce) jar roasted red peppers

1/4 cup white wine

4 cups chicken broth

1/3 cup blue cheese stuffed green olives

1 teaspoon Spanish smoked paprika

1 teaspoon salt + pepper to taste

Pinch of saffron

16-ounce fresh seafood (your choice of any seafood)

Juice of 2 lemons

Fresh parsley, for serving

White truffle oil, for serving (optional)

Directions:

1. Chop the onion and mince the garlic. Slice the chorizo, parsley, and red peppers. Chop the tomatoes. Preheat your grill to high heat.

2. Put a big cast iron skillet on the grill. Let it heat up until it's hot. Then put in the olive oil, garlic, and onions. Add a little salt and pepper, and let everything cook for 3 to 5 minutes. Stir frequently until the onions become soft. Then put in the chorizo until it becomes brown, around 2 to 3 minutes. Put in the red peppers and the tomatoes as well as any of their juice. Let everything cook for 5 more minutes.

3. Pour in the wine and deglaze the skillet. Once deglazed, add in the rice, and stir to combine. Continue to cook for 3 to 5 minutes, until the rice is toasted. Stir in the chicken broth slowly. Put in the olives, a little more salt, and pepper, chicken, paprika, and saffron. Stir everything together, and cover the skillet. Cook for 15 minutes covered.

4.   While cooking, mix the seafood with salt and pepper, and olive oil. When the 15 minutes are up and in the seafood, and cover again. Cook for about another 15 minutes. The dish is ready when the seafood is completely cooked.

5.   Top the paella with freshly squeezed lemon juice, and garnish with parsley, and white truffle oil if desired. Salt and pepper to taste, and serve.

Nutritional Info: Calories: 561 | Sodium: 1492 mg | Dietary Fiber: 1.9 g |
Total Fat: 18.1 g | Total Carbs: 57.1 g | Protein: 37.0 g

Squid with Ginger Soy Sauce

Servings: 4 | Prep Time: 20 Minutes | Cook Time: 4 Minutes

This dish is a popular Asian street food. It has a lovely fragrant smell, and full flavor.

Ingredients:

    1/2 cup soy sauce

    2 tablespoons grated fresh ginger

    3 tablespoons mirin

    1 pound small squid (bodies and tentacles)

Directions:

1. Clean the squid. Preheat your grill to high heat.

2. Combine the ginger, mirin, and soy sauce in a big bowl. Take out 1/2 cup and save it for later.

3. Put the squid in the rest of the mixture, and coat it with it. Turn in over in the mixture 4 times.

4. Then let it rest for 10 minutes, flipping it over once halfway through.

5. Cook the squid for about 4 minutes. Turn it over every 30 seconds, and coat it with the saved marinade. The squid will be white when it's ready.

6. Serve immediately.

Nutritional Info: Calories: 149 | Sodium: 1945 mg | Dietary Fiber: 0.6 g |
Total Fat: 1.7 g | Total Carbs: 13.1 g | Protein: 19.9 g

Sun Dried Tomato Spinach Pesto Grilled Cheese

Servings: 8 | Prep Time: 7 Minutes | Cook Time: 8 Minutes

This grilled cheese sandwich isn't your average grilled cheese. The flavors of the pesto, and sun dried tomatoes combine to create a sweet and savory treat.

Ingredients:

16 slices sourdough bread

8 tablespoons pesto sauce

6-ounce sun dried tomatoes

4 – 6 ounces fresh spinach

8 slices provolone cheese

2 – 4 tablespoons olive oil

Directions:

1. Preheat your grill to medium heat.

2. Coat one side of the slice of bread with olive oil. Slice the cheese slices in half.

3. Spread the pesto on the uncoated side of 8 pieces of bread.

4. Top the pesto with 1 slice of cheese, then the sun dried tomatoes, then the spinach, and another slice of cheese.

5. Top with another slice of bread with the olive oil side facing out.

6. Grill the sandwiches for 2 to 4 minutes a side. The cheese will be melty when sandwiches are done.

Nutritional Info: Calories: 419 | Sodium: 774 mg | Dietary Fiber: 2.5 g |
Total Fat: 22.2 g | Total Carbs: 39.3 g | Protein: 17.0 g

Matt Jason

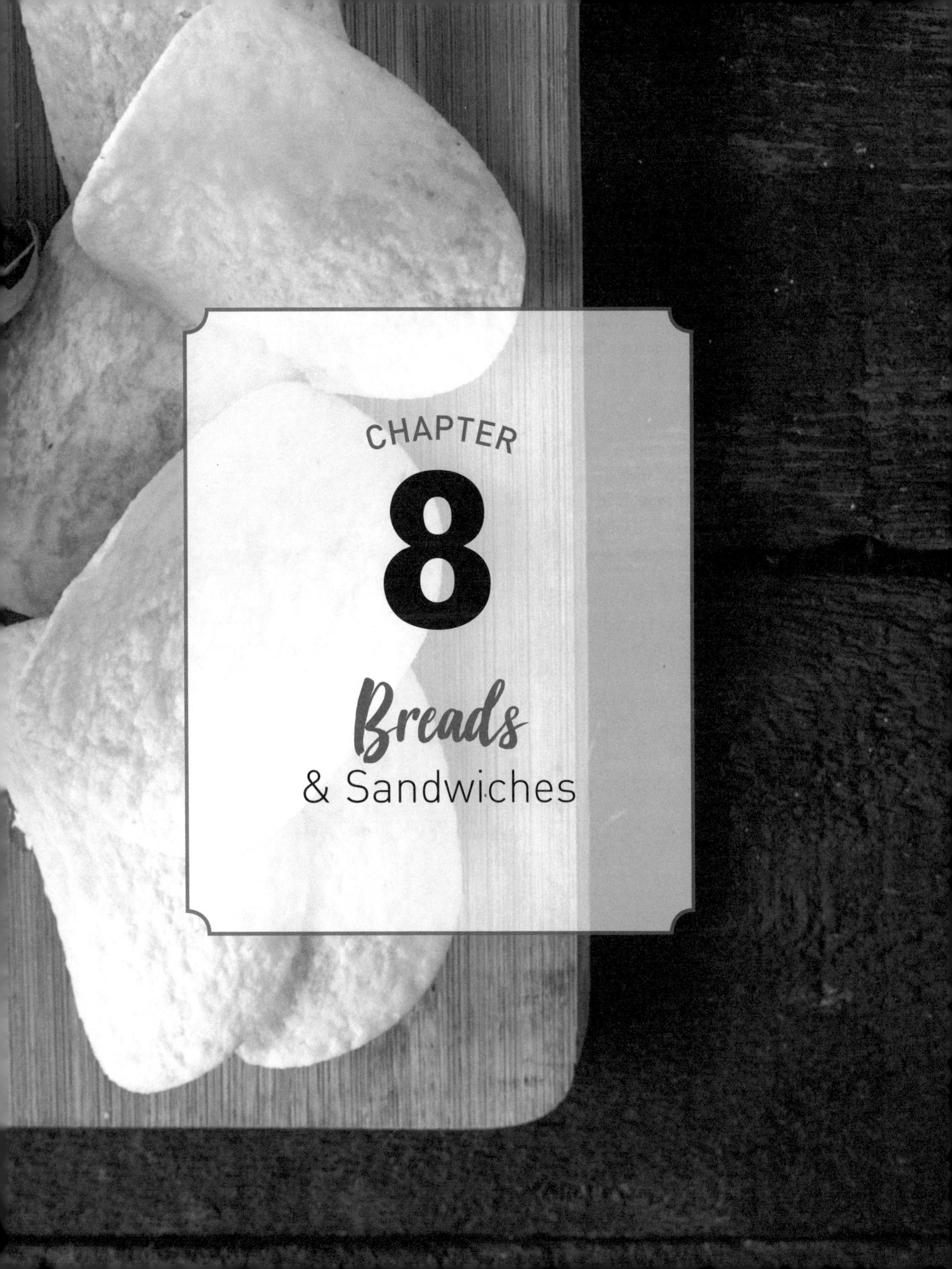

CHAPTER 8

Breads & Sandwiches

Grilled Angel Food Cake with Strawberry Rhubarb Sauce

Servings: 6 Servings | Prep Time: 10 Minutes | Cook Time: 9 Minutes

Grilling the angel food cake gives a savory dimension to this light, airy cake. This makes the perfect dessert to a summer barbeque.

Ingredients:

1 1/2 cups strawberries, chopped

3/4 cups chopped rhubarb

1/2 cup sugar

6 tablespoons water

1 3/4 teaspoons vanilla

1/8 teaspoon cinnamon

1 store bought angel food cake, cut into 6 pieces

3/4 cups whipped topping

Directions:

1. Chop the strawberries, and rhubarb. Slice the angel food cake into 6 pieces.

2. Combine all the ingredients EXCEPT for the cake, and whipped topping in a saucepan. Heat on medium heat for 5 minutes, the mixture should be just about to boil. Set aside for later.

3. Preheat your grill on medium heat.

4. Grill the angel food cake for about 2 minutes a side. The cake should be lightly toasted on both sides.

5. Plate the cake, and top with the sauce. Serve with whipped topping on the side.

Nutritional Info: Calories: 146 | Sodium: 645 mg | Dietary Fiber: 2.6 g | Total Fat: 4.7 g | Total Carbs: 5.5 g | Protein: 22.3 g

Grilled Bread with Prosciutto

Servings: 6 | Prep Time: 10 Minutes | Cook Time: 5 Minutes

This simple dish is filled with flavor. It gets saltiness from the prosciutto, creaminess from the cheese, and savory from the garlic.

Ingredients:

6 slices good Tuscan round bread

1 large garlic clove

High-quality olive oil

2 ounces thinly sliced prosciutto

2-ounce fresh smoked mozzarella

3 tablespoons fresh parsley

Kosher salt and freshly ground black pepper

Directions:

1. Preheat your grill to medium heat. Cut the garlic clove in half. Mince the parsley. Grate the mozzarella. Slice the bread 3/4-inch thick. Tear the prosciutto into smaller pieces.

2. Grill one side of the bread for 2 minutes. It will be golden when ready.

3. Run the cut side of the garlic on the grilled side of the bread. Coat the grilled side of the bread with 1 tablespoon olive oil. Top with the prosciutto, and then the cheese.

4. Put the bread back on the grill for 1 to 2 more minutes. The bread is ready when the cheese starts to melt.

5. Top with a little olive oil, parsley, and salt and pepper to taste.

Nutritional Info: Calories: 71 | Sodium: 261 mg | Dietary Fiber: 0 g |
Total Fat: 4.7 g | Total Carbs: 2.6 g | Protein: 5.7 g

Grilled Pound Cake with Chocolate Sauce and Whipped Cream

Servings: 8 | Prep Time: 10 Minutes | Cook Time: 6 Minutes

Grilling the pound cake gives it a nice smoky flavor the compliments its sweetness. The chocolate sauce and whipped cream gives this dish a wonderful richness.

Ingredients:

- 1 3/4 cups heavy cream, divided
- 1 tablespoon light corn starch
- 4 ounces high-quality dark chocolate
- 1/4 cup butter
- 1-pound cake
- 2 tablespoons sugar

Directions:

1. Cut the chocolate into small pieces. Set the butter out to soften. Cut the pound cake into 1-inch slices. Preheat your grill to medium heat.

2. Place 3/4 cups heavy cream in a sauce pan, and heat on medium heat. Bring the cream to a boil and then turn off the heat and put in the corn starch. Remove the pan from the heat, and mix in the chocolate until the sauce is smooth.

3. Use a whisk to whip the sugar and remaining cream until it becomes firm.

4. Coat the pound cake with a light coating of butter on both sides. Grill the pound cake for 1 minute a side.

5. Top the pound cake with chocolate sauce, and serve with whipped cream on the side.

Nutritional Info: Calories: 444 | Sodium: 257 mg | Dietary Fiber: 0.7 g |
Total Fat: 27.9 g | Total Carbs: 46.6 g | Protein: 3.7 g

Naan Caprese Pizza

Servings: 2 | Prep Time: 5 Minutes | Cook Time: 16 Minutes

Naan is a traditional Indian that has a nice buttery flavor. It lends itself well to creamy fresh flavors of the caprese.

Ingredients:

    1/4 cup balsamic vinegar

    2 naan

    Cooking spray

    A handful or two of cherry or grape tomatoes, halved

    A handful or two of small fresh mozzarella balls (ciliegine)

    1/4 cup fresh basil ribbons

    Salt and pepper to taste

Directions:

1. Preheat your grill to medium-high heat. Halve the tomatoes.

2. Put the balsamic vinegar in a saucepan and heat on medium heat. Simmer for around 8 - 10 minutes until the vinegar has reduced in size to around a tablespoon.

3. Lightly spray both sides of the naan with cooking spray. Grill for 2 to 3 minutes a side. Both sides should be slightly charred.

4. Combine the cheese, basil, and tomatoes on top of the naan. Top with the balsamic, and salt and pepper to taste. Serve immediately.

Nutritional Info: Calories: 94 | Sodium: 169 mg | Dietary Fiber: 0.8 g | Total Fat: 0.9 g | Total Carbs: 16.4 g | Protein: 3.5 g

Pantry

- **HERBS** – If we were to go through every cooking herb there was this would be a very long book which is why they are all compiled under a single name. It is always good to keep some of your more traditional dried herbs on hand like rosemary, thyme, oregano, and parsley.

- **SALT AND PEPPER** – This one may sound like a no-brainer, but sometimes a nice steak only needs a little salt and pepper to really stand out.

- **ONIONS** – Onions are great because they last forever in the pantry and can be used in so many ways. The George Foreman grill makes perfect grilled onions that compliment any steak or burger.

- **BREAD AND BUNS** – These are probably going to be in your pantry anyway, but having a variety of bread and buns at your disposal is great for cooking all kinds of sandwiches.

- **DRY RUBS AND OTHER SPICES** – Dry rubs and other spice concoctions never really go bad so they are perfect to collect in your pantry. A simple dry rub can do wonders for a cut of meat and the more you have the more options you have.

UMAMI *Fifth flavor*

Often called the "fifth flavor" after sweet, salty, sour, and bitter, umami can best be described as savory, but what does savory taste like? In Japanese, umami translates to "a pleasant savory taste." Scientifically, umami is determined by the amount of glutamate in a particular food. (Think of it as a natural way of getting a flavor boost similar to MSG). The amazing thing about umami is that it can be found in all kinds of foods. Try adding a pinch of one of these ingredients to almost any recipe. **Often the taste is amazing!**

Vegetables/Plants

Seaweed (kombu and nori) | **Soybean products** (Soy sauce, miso, tofu) | **Tomatoes** | **Green teas** | **Kimchi** (Korean fermented vegetables) | **Mushrooms**

Meats

Bacon | Ham | Pork | Beef | Chicken | Eggs

Seafood

Sardines | Bonito (Dried fish flakes) | Tuna | Mackerel | Shrimp | Anchovies | Oysters | Mussels | Caviar and other fish eggs

Cheeses

Parmesan | Comte/Gruyere | Roquefort | Gouda | Cheddar

Flavor Building

The best way to start building flavors is with a general seasoning with salt and black pepper. You can also experiment with these herbs and spices to build fun, new flavors with different proteins.

BEEF	SALMON	PORK	CHICKEN	VEGETABLES
Shallots	Lemon Pepper	Mustard	Rosemary	Olive Oil
Garlic	Citrus	Thyme	Garlic	Thyme
Thyme	Paprika	White Wine	White Wine	Mint
Cumin	Dill	Apple Cider	Thyme	Onion Powder
Rosemary	Basil	Rosemary	Soy Sauce	
Red Wine	Olive Oil		Lemon Pepper	
			Olive Oil	

Wine and Beer Pairing

Try these varieties with your favorite meats and fish.

NEW YORK OR RIBEYE STEAKS

Wine	Beer
Cabernet Sauvignon	IPA
Malbec	Brown Ale
Shiraz	Stout

SALMON

Wine	Beer
Sauvignon Blanc	Pilsner
Pinot Grigio	Lager
Riesling	IPA

PORK

Wine	Beer
Chardonnay	Brown Ale
Pinot Noir	IPA
	Stout

WHITE FISHES

Wine	Beer
Sauvignon Blanc	Light Ale
Chardonnay	Pilsner
	Hefeweissen

CHICKEN

Wine	Beer
Sauvignon Blanc	Pilsner
Merlot	Lager
Pinot Noir	Light Ale

10 CLASSIC Salad Dressings

Ranch
 mayonnaise   buttermilk   chives   dill   onion powder   garlic powder   salt   black pepper

Caesar
 canola oil   parmesan cheese   anchovy   fresh garlic   egg yolk   black pepper

Bleu Cheese
 blue cheese   buttermilk   sour cream   mayonnaise   white wine vinegar   sugar   garlic powder   black pepper

Thousand Islands
 mayonnaise   ketchup   white vinegar   sugar   sweet pickle relish   salt   black pepper

Italian
 olive oil   white or red wine vinegar   garlic powder   oregano   dried basil   onion powder   crushed red pepper   salt   black pepper   lemon juice

Balsamic Vinaigrette
 balsamic vinegar   honey   dijon mustard   olive oil   garlic   salt   black pepper

Honey Mustard
 dijon mustard   honey   apple cider vinegar   salt   vegetable oil

Greek
 red wine vinegar   olive oil   lemon juice   dried oregano   salt   black pepper

French
 vegetable oil   ketchup   sugar   white vinegar   water   garlic powder   salt   black pepper

Russian
 onion   mayonnaise   ketchup   horseradish   hot sauce   worcestershire sauce   paprika   salt

10 CLASSIC Sauces

Bordelaise
 red wine | shallots | dried thyme | bay leaf | beef stock | salt | black pepper

Hollandaise
 egg yolks | lemon juice | butter | salt

Mayonnaise
 egg yolks | dry mustard | sugar | lemon juice | white wine vinegar | vegetable oil | salt

Buffalo
 Hot sauce (like Frank's Red Hot) | butter | vinegar | Worcestershire sauce | garlic powder

Italian Tomato
 tomatoes | onions | garlic | olive oil | basil | oregano | salt | black pepper

Chimichurri
 fresh parsley | garlic | oregano | olive oil | white wine vinegar | salt | black pepper

Salsa Verde
 tomatillos | onion | serrano chile | garlic | cilantro | vegetable oil | salt

Alfredo
 butter | heavy cream | garlic | Parmesan cheese | parsley

Bechamel
 milk | butter | flour | salt

Barbecue
 ketchup | apple juice | apple cider vinegar | brown sugar | butter | chili powder | garlic | onion | salt

A FUNCTIONAL PANTRY:

If you are going to cook a wide variety of dishes, you will need to have certain ingredients on-hand at all times. Keep your pantry well stocked with these ingredients:

All-purpose flour: Good for general baking and other kitchen uses

Baking powder: A double acting leavening agent that is needed for most baking

Baking soda: A leavening agent that is used when there are acidic ingredients

Kosher salt: less harsh tasting than table salt and good for cooking

Black pepper: used for seasoning before and after cooking

Olive oil: flavorful and good for low-temperature cooking and salad dressings

Vinegars: white, apple cider, white wine, red wine, and balsamic

Baking chocolate: good for a variety of desserts

Vanilla extract: flavorful addition to baked goods

White sugar: needed for most types of baking

Brown sugar: needed for many types of cakes, cookies, as well as savory dishes

Honey: a great natural sweetener

Long grain white rice: great as a light side dish

Brown rice: a healthier alternative to white rice

Breadcrumbs: handy for baking and frying

Stocks: chicken, beef, and vegetable for sauces, stews, and additional flavor

Beans: high in protein and fiber and useful in many dishes

Dry herbs and spices: bay leaves, cayenne pepper, chili powder, cinnamon, cloves, crushed red pepper, cumin, curry powder, fennel seed, garlic, ginger, nutmeg, oregano, paprika (sweet and smoked), rosemary, thyme

Dairy: milk, salted and unsalted butter, eggs, plain yogurt

Cheeses: cheddar, Parmesan, goat cheese, low moisture mozzarella

HOW TO CHOOSE VEGETABLES:

Leafy greens
Look for greens that are green all over. Otherwise, they may be starting to rot.

Tomatoes
Avoid bruised or discolored tomatoes. Tomatoes sold on the vine typically last longer than those sold without the vine.

Potatoes
Avoid potatoes that have a slight greenish hue. Look for potatoes that do not have any deep scars or large bruises.

Carrots
Look for carrots that have a healthy orange color and fresh-looking greens.

Peppers
Peppers should be free from bruises and their skin should be smooth and not wrinkly. Also look for healthy looking stems.

Mushrooms
Look for firm, fresh, smooth appearance. If the cap is closed underneath the flavor will be delicate. If it is open and you can see the gills it will have richer flavor. Fresh herbs: Herbs will last longer if they have the roots attached. After buying fresh herbs, put them in a glass of water to help them stay fresh longer.

HOW TO CHOOSE MEATS:

Beef

Most beef is either "choice" or "prime." Prime has the highest fat content, but it is also very expensive. If you can afford prime, it's the best, but most choice beef is quite good as well. When shopping for beef, look for marbling (the more the better) and try to find beef that has a healthy red color.

Grain fed or grass fed?
Most beef in the United States is grain fed, and this is what Americans are used to eating. Grass fed beef has a stronger flavor and often a higher fat content. A lot of grass-fed beef is grain fed and then finished on grass.

Pork

Pork comes in many varieties, and again, freshness is key. Pork chops should be a light pink color with small ribbons of fat through the meat. Always look for well-marbled pork. When buying pork loins and tenderloins, look for pieces that have been well trimmed. Otherwise, you end up paying for fat you will throw away. When buying bacon, avoid those containing a lot of sugar in the dry rub.

Fresh fish

Fresh fish—meaning it has not been frozen—is always better. It will have a better texture and fresher flavor. When buying salmon, look for fish with high fat content. This will make the meat juicier. Also, make sure your salmon has a sweet smell and not a fishy smell. Ahi tuna should be deep red in color and should have almost no smell at all. Also, look for well-trimmed tuna that has had the bloodline removed. White fishes like flounder, halibut, cod, and sole should have a slightly sweet smell and slick, not dry, looking flesh.

Chicken

When buying chicken, it's all about freshness. Fresh chicken should have very little smell and the skin should be a healthy yellowish color. Commercial chicken is often pre-brined, meaning it has been injected with salt water. While brining a chicken before cooking is a great way to improve flavor and moisture, avoid pre-brined chicken because you will end up paying for water. Also avoid chicken raised with any kind of hormones. When selecting a whole chicken, try to find one that is between four and five pounds for best flavor and texture.

Shellfish

Avoid buying frozen shellfish. It will have a mushy texture and slightly sulfurous smell. When buying oysters, try to buy local because oysters are sold live. For lobsters and crabs, live-bought is best. Otherwise, they can have a fishy smell. Pre-cooked lobsters and crab often become overcooked when reheated.

WAYS TO COOK *Vegetables*   # WAYS TO COOK *Meat*

ASPARAGUS		
Steam	Roast at	Grill
10 min	350 - 10 min	5 min

NY STEAK/RIBEYE	
Broil	Grill
4 min per side	4 min per side

CARROTS		
Steam	Roast at	Grill
15 min	350 - 20 min	10 min

FILET MIGNON	
Broil	Grill
5 min per side	5-6 min per side

POTATOES		
Steam	Roast at	Grill
20 min	350 - 40 min	15 min

TRI TIP	
Roast at	Grill
375 - 40 min	25-30 min

ZUCCHINI		
Steam	Roast at	Grill
10 min	350 - 20 min	10 min

CHICKEN (WHOLE)	
Roast at	Grill
375 - 90 min	90 min

BELL PEPPERS		
Steam	Roast at	Grill
5 min	350 - 10 min	5 min

CHICKEN (BREAST)	
Sautee	Grill
8 min per side	5-6 min per side

GREEN BEANS		
Steam	Roast at	Grill
5 min	350 - 15 min	Do not grill

CHICKEN (THIGHS)	
Roast at	Grill
375 - 30 min	15-20 min

BROCCOLI		
Steam	Roast at	Grill
10 min	350 - 15 min	10 min

PORK CHOPS	
Sautee	Grill
5 min per side	5 min per side

CAULIFLOWER		
Steam	Roast at	Grill
10 min	350 - 15 min	10 min

PORK TENDERLOIN	
Roast at	Grill
350 - 20 min	12-15 min

HOW LONG DOES FOOD LAST IN THE FREEZER? (RAW UNLESS STATED OTHERWISE)

Meat, poultry, eggs & seafood

Beef/Lamb/Pork	4 to 12 months
Ham (cooked)	1 to 2 months
Ham	6 months
Chicken/turkey	9 months
Eggs	DO NOT FREEZE EGGS
Chicken nuggets	1 to 3 months
Hamburger patties	3 to 4 months
Hot dogs	1 to 2 months
Lean fish	6 months
Fatty fish	2 to 3 months
Shellfish	3 to 6 months

Produce

Fruit (except bananas)	10 to 12 months
Bananas	3 months
Citrus fruit	4 to 6 months
Most vegetables	8 to 10 months
Tomatoes	2 months

Dairy

Ice Cream	1 to 2 months
Butter	6 to 9 months

Other

Soup/stew	2 to 3 months
Fruit juice	8 to 12 months
Cake	4 to 6 months
Cookies (baked)	3 months
Cookie dough	2 months
Pies (baked)	2 to 4 months
Pies (unbaked)	8 months

KITCHEN UNIT CONVERSION

1 teaspoon	= 1/3 tbsp =	4.9 ml
1 dessertspoon	= 2 tsp =	9.9 ml
1 tablespoon	= 1.5 dstsp / 3 tsp =	14.8 ml
1 fuid ounce	= 2 tbsp / 6 tsp =	29.6 ml
1 cup	= 16 tbsp / 48 tsp =	236.6 ml
1 quart	= 4 cup =	946 ml
1 gal	= 4 quart / 16 cup =	3.79 l
1 ounce	= 2 tbsp =	28.4 g
1 pounds	= 16 oz =	453.6 g

Want a Personal 24/7 Cooking Coach?

Learn New Recipes & Techniques for FREE!

Made in United States
Cleveland, OH
02 December 2024

11217286R00081